BOOK-KEEPING

APPLIED TO

AGRICULTURE,

MANUFACTURES, COMMERCE,

BANKING, AND EXCHANGE.

BY

IRA MAYHEW.

BOSTON:
SAMUEL F. NICHOLS,

MAYHEW'S

PRACTICAL BOOK-KEEPING

EMBRACING

SINGLE AND DOUBLE ENTRY,

COMMERCIAL CALCULATIONS, AND THE PHILOSOPHY AND MORALS OF BUSINESS.

"Deliver all things in number and weight, and put all in writing that thou givest out or receivest in." Ecclesiasticus xlii. 7.

BY IRA MAYHEW, A. M.,

AUTHOR OF "MEANS AND ENDS OF UNIVERSAL EDUCATION."

BOSTON:

SAMUEL F. NICHOLS,

43 WASHINGTON STREET.

1866.

ACCOUNT BOOKS.

A SET of Account Books has been prepared expressly to accompany this volume, of sufficient size and properly ruled for writing up all the Examples for Practice it contains, consisting of

I. A LEDGER FOR THE FIRST FORM OF ACCOUNTS. One Book.
II. A LEDGER FOR THE SECOND FORM OF ACCOUNTS. One Book.
III. A DAY BOOK AND LEDGER FOR THE THIRD FORM OF ACCOUNTS. Two Books.
IV. A JOURNAL AND LEDGER FOR DOUBLE ENTRY. Two Books.

These Account Books cost but little more than common paper.

KEY TO BOOK-KEEPING.

A KEY to this Book-keeping has been prepared, in which all the *Examples for Practice* occurring in the Book-keeping are carefully written out, and in which the more difficult of the *Commercial Calculations* are made. The Key will be of advantage to Teachers in testing the accuracy of the work of classes, and may be of service to the private learner.

PRINTED BY
GEO. C. RAND & AVERY.

ELECTROTYPED AT THE
BOSTON STEREOTYPE FOUNDRY.

FROM PREFACE TO FIRST EDITION.

AGESILAUS, king of Sparta, being asked what things he thought most proper for *boys to learn*, very appropriately replied, "Those things which they should *practice* when they become men." Ever since it was said to Adam, "In the sweat of thy face shalt thou eat bread," there has been a necessity laid upon man not only to *labor*, but to EXCHANGE *with others the products of his industry*, in order to obtain a comfortable support. "Deliver all things in number and weight, and put all in writing that thou givest out or receivest in," is a precept of universal application; and there is a special necessity for its observance in all business transactions between debtor and creditor. . . . Considerations are presented in the Introduction to show some of the many advantages that would result to individuals and to the community from making Bookkeeping a common study in all our schools. . . .

PREFACE TO THE SIXTIETH EDITION.

Since the first publication of this work, in 1851, the author and publishers have received many testimonials in its favor, the strongest and most cordial of which have been from *teachers who have used it.* These testimonials are from public and private school teachers, from the principals and teachers of academies and ladies' seminaries, from professors and teachers in state normal schools, from presidents and professors of colleges, both literary and commercial, and from city and state superintendents of schools, to whom — and especially to a few who have kindly suggested slight modifications in the text — the author would render grateful acknowledgments.

The present *Revised Edition* it is hoped will be found more worthy of patronage. Part Second and Part Third are entirely new.

IRA MAYHEW.

ALBION, MICH., 1860.

CONTENTS.

TO THE STUDENT.

From an attentive perusal of the following Introduction, you will see some of the many benefits resulting to persons engaged in the various departments of productive industry, from the study and practice of Book-keeping. Others will present themselves to your mind in your progress through the book. While you can gain nothing by leaving a subject imperfectly understood, you will lose much. You should hence let it be a settled rule with you never to proceed onward while any thing remains unconquered behind. In order, then, to facilitate your progress in this important study, and to render it of the greatest practical utility, you will do well constantly to bear in mind the following suggestions, until you shall have formed correct *habits* in relation to the several particulars named:—

1. Make every arithmetical calculation yourself, as you proceed. Rely not upon any result stated in the book, until you have first made the computation on which it depends; otherwise, although the *author* may have derived some discipline from its preparation, *you* certainly will gain little from its perusal. What is worth doing at all, is worth doing well.

2. In solving the Examples for Practice, exercise your *common sense* in determining how each transaction is to be entered; whether all on one side of the account, and if so, on which; or a part on one side of the account and a part on the other. Bear in mind, also, that a transaction will sometimes require an entry to each of several accounts.

3. Spell every word correctly, and write neatly and legibly.

4. Study brevity and perspicuity in recording business transactions, and in all your business correspondence.

5. Accuracy in accounts is a cardinal virtue. It is less difficult to fall into errors than to *correct* them. Therefore,

6. Exercise all diligence to keep your Account Books neat, legible, promptly written up, and free from errors.

ABBREVIATIONS AND SIGNS.

Acct. . . . . Account.
Amt. . . . . Amount.
Ans. . . . . Answer.
Apr. . . . . April.
Aug. . . . . August.
B. or *Bk.* . . Bank.
Bal. . . . . Balance.
Bbl. . . . . . Barrel.
B. B. . . . . Bill Book, *or* Bank Book.
B. P. . . . . Bills Payable.
B. R . . . . Bills Receivable.
Bush. . . . . Bushel.
C. or *Ct.* . . Cent.
Cash. . . . . Cashier.
C. B. . . . . Cash Book.
Cent. . . . . (Centum) A hundred.
Clk. . . . . Clerk.
Co. . . . . . Company.
Cr. . . . . . Creditor.
Cwt. . . . . Hundred Weight.
D. or *d.* . . . Day.
D. B. . . . . Day Book.
Dec. . . . . December.
Dis. . . . . Discount.
Do. . . . . . (Ditto) The Same.
Dolls. . . . Dollars.
Doz. . . . . Dozen.
D. P. . . . . Day Book Page.
Dr. . . . . . Debtor.
E. E. . . . . Errors Excepted.
E. and *O. E.* Errors and Omissions [Excepted.
Ex. . . . . . Example.
Exs. . . . . Expenses.
Fav. . . . . Favor.
Feb. . . . . February.
Frt. . . . . Freight.
Ft. . . . . . Foot, *or* Feet.
Gal. . . . . Gallon.
Hdkf. . . . . Handkerchief.
Hhd. . . . . Hogshead.
Hund. . . . Hundred.
I. or *Inv.* . . Invoice.
I. B. . . . . Invoice Book.
i. e. . . . . . That is.
Ins. . . . . Insurance.
Int. . . . . Interest.
Invt. . . . . Inventory.
J. P. . . . . Journal Page.
Jan. . . . . January.
L. F. . . . . Ledger Folio.
M. or *mo.* . . Month.
Mar. . . . . March.
Mdse. . . . . Merchandise.
No. . . . . . Number.
Nov. . . . . November.
Oct. . . . . October.
P. or *p.* . . . Page.
Payt. . . . . Payment.
Pd. . . . . . Paid.
Pkg. . . . . Package.
Per or *pr.* . By the.
Per an. . . . By the year.
P and *L.* . . Profit and Loss.
Pr. . . . . . Pair.
Prem. . . . Premium.
Ps. . . . . . Piece, *or* Pieces.
Pres. . . . . President.
Prin. . . . . Principal.
S. B. . . . . Sales Book.
Sec. . . . . Secretary.
Sept. . . . . September.
Stg. . . . . Sterling.
Sunds. . . . Sundries.
Tr. . . . . . Transaction.
Viz. . . . . To wit; namely.
Y. or *yr.* . . Year.
Yds. . . . . Yards.

+, *plus* . . . Addition.
—, *minus* . . Subtraction.
=, *equal* . . Equality.
×, *into* . . . Multiplication.
÷, *by* . . . . Division.
: *is to,* } . . Proportion.
: : *as,* } . . 3 : 12 : : 5 : 20.
$ . . . . . . Dollars.
¢ . . . . . . Cents.
£ . . . . . . Pounds Sterling.
@ . . . . . . At, or to.
% . . . . . Per cent.
" . . . . . The same.
1^1 . . . . . . One and 1-quarter.
1^2 . . . . . . One and 1-half.
1^3 . . . . . . One and 3-quarters.

SUGGESTIONS TO TEACHERS.

BOOK-KEEPING has not heretofore been a common branch of study in our schools, and teachers introducing it will hence often have occasion to instruct classes in what they have not themselves been taught. But this work, which has been prepared with reference thereto, and which assumes nothing as known that is not taught, while simple and progressive, is yet practical and thorough. Great care has been taken to render the more difficult parts of the science clear and intelligible. Teachers of capacity and industry may hence as readily prepare themselves for giving instruction in it, with entire success, as in any other branch of study.

The accompanying Account Books have been prepared with proper rulings, and of sufficient capacity for writing up the Examples for Practice in the various forms of account, introduced on pp. 60, 77, 105, and 198. The Illustrative Examples which precede, may be worked out on separate sheets of paper, ruled by the pupil as the several forms require. It will be well, also, for the learner thus to work out the Examples for Practice in the different forms of account, before entering them in the Account Books.

Although Keys are not generally desirable, still, in works constructed like this they seem unavoidable. The Key to this treatise, which contains the writing up of all the Examples for Practice introduced into the book, with the solution of the more difficult examples in Commercial Calculations, will enable teachers who might otherwise shrink from the undertaking, to study and teach this important science with great satisfaction, both to themselves and to their pupils and patrons.

SUGGESTIONS TO TEACHERS.

BOOK-KEEPING has not heretofore been a common branch of study in our schools, and teachers introducing it will hence often have occasion to instruct classes in what they have not themselves been taught. But this work, which has been prepared with reference thereto, and which assumes nothing as known that is not taught, while simple and progressive, is yet practical and thorough. Great care has been taken to render the more difficult parts of the science clear and intelligible. Teachers of capacity and industry may hence as readily prepare themselves for giving instruction in it, with entire success, as in any other branch of study.

The accompanying Account Books have been prepared with proper rulings, and of sufficient capacity for writing up the Examples for Practice in the various forms of account, introduced on pp. 60, 77, 105, and 198. The Illustrative Examples which precede, may be worked out on separate sheets of paper, ruled by the pupil as the several forms require. It will be well, also, for the learner thus to work out the Examples for Practice in the different forms of account, before entering them in the Account Books.

Although Keys are not generally desirable, still, in works constructed like this they seem unavoidable. The Key to this treatise, which contains the writing up of all the Examples for Practice introduced into the book, with the solution of the more difficult examples in Commercial Calculations, will enable teachers who might otherwise shrink from the undertaking, to study and teach this important science with great satisfaction, both to themselves and to their pupils and patrons.

how, or for what, money or property has come into their possession. It can hardly be set down as uncharitable to infer that such love darkness rather than light, because their deeds are evil, and fear the light of correct entries, lest their deeds should be reproved. It must be apparent to every one, that all such persons need the *restraints* imposed by keeping an exact account of receipts and disbursements. Book-keeping, then, should be studied in every common school in the country, (as well as in all our higher seminaries of learning,) by young persons of both sexes.

4. Heretofore Book-keeping has rarely been studied, except by young men who have expected to engage in mercantile and commercial pursuits. But were it understood and practiced by women as well as by men, it would in many cases (and very properly too) render them more frugal in their personal and domestic expenses; prevent vast accumulations of indebtedness; diminish greatly the number of bankruptcies in the country; and secure to families generally the benefits resulting from living within their means. It would, moreover, exert a healthful influence upon the mind, and afford rational employment for many upon whom time hangs heavily, or is worse than thrown away in idleness and thoughtless dissipation.

5. While upon the husband, father, or brother, rests the duty of providing for the necessities, comforts, and conveniences of the family — upon the wife, daughter, or sister, devolves the scarcely less responsible office of judiciously expending the means furnished, in so far at least as the well-being of the household requires. This is by common consent regarded as coming within her appropriate sphere. It is, then, properly a part of the housewife's business to keep an account of all moneys expended by her for the benefit of

QUEST. 4. What benefits would result to women and families from this study? — **5.** State benefits at length, from keeping household accounts.

the family, or on its behalf. When she does this, she becomes more fully a *helpmeet* for man, than it is possible for her otherwise to be. Domestic broils and family feuds not unfrequently result, either from real or supposed scanty provision on the part of the husband, or from alleged extravagance on the part of the wife. In case an account of the family expenses is kept as here suggested, the wife can at any time render an account for all moneys that have passed through her hands. Where the husband keeps a proper account of his business, it is hence easy to see when it may become necessary to curtail expenses in order to live within their means. It is evident, moreover, that under such circumstances two whose destinies are united for life, can more rationally confer together in relation to the well-being of the household, than where no such accounts are kept. I may here also venture one additional suggestion intimately connected with the preceding.

6. The wife or daughter might, in many instances, very properly keep the books of the husband or father, whose time is absorbed in the pursuits of a laborious profession, and thus not only save the expense of a clerk, but transact the business of the household more satisfactorily, and have the pleasure of contributing to the comfort and happiness of the family, as well as to its pecuniary interests. Woman, when not otherwise employed, may also properly enter the counting-room, and engage with father and brothers in its quiet duties, for the discharge of which she is as well fitted by nature as they. She thus acquires a knowledge of business, and if bereft of husband or father, upon whom too many females are entirely dependent for support, she may be enabled herself to conduct the business advantageously, or to close it without loss.

QUEST. 6. How may women aid in business by keeping books? What of woman in the counting-room? May she learn to conduct a business herself?

7. Females, as heretofore generally educated, have been quite too dependent for a support upon their male relatives and friends, if such they chance to have. Frequently, too frequently, alas! there is exhibited the painful spectacle of the *widow*, bereft of him to whom she has been accustomed to look for support and the maintenance of her little ones, without any knowledge of the ordinary forms of business, and hence not only without the means of procuring a competency for herself and children, but unable advantageously to assume the charge of any property she may chance to possess. Under such circumstances, few females, comparatively, are prepared properly to conduct their own business. Losses, embarrassments, poverty, and not unfrequently the painful sense of dependence upon the cold charities of an unfeeling world, hasten those thus situated, who but yesterday were confiding and full of hope, *on* to a premature death, leaving the world sorrowful and broken-hearted, chiefly because of a defective education. How important it is, then, that the study under consideration should receive the attention of females as well as of males! Especially should Book-keeping be regarded as an indispensable study in every young ladies' seminary.

8. The one great object which parents seek to attain in directing their children to enter upon the study of Arithmetic in our schools, and which youth have in view in entering upon it, is, that they may become the better qualified for the discharge of the ordinary duties of life and for the transaction of such business as they may have occasion to engage in. But if a portion of the time ordinarily given to this study were judiciously bestowed upon a practical system of General Book-keeping, this important object would be much more

QUEST. **7.** In case of bereavement, which is better, for widow and orphan to be able to conduct the business of the husband and father, or to depend upon friends? Should ladies learn Book-keeping? — **8.** Is this study of less importance than Arithmetic?

speedily reached, and with vastly more pleasure to the learner.

9. I would not underrate the importance of arithmetic as a study in our primary institutions of learning. It has long and very properly been pursued, in all well regulated schools, by both boys and girls, whose education would be exceedingly defective without a familiar acquaintance with its principles and their application to the ordinary transactions of life. But it is apparent that a practical familiarity with the principles of General Book-keeping is of much greater importance than the most perfect comprehension of the mysteries of square and cube root, of arithmetical and geometrical progression, of permutations and combinations, of the summation of an infinite series, etc., to say nothing of the exploded rules of single and double position, and many others that might be enumerated.

10. English Grammar, which is defined as the art of speaking and writing the English language with propriety and accuracy, is now very generally studied in our common schools. But in order to turn it to the greatest account, its principles should be practically applied, *in the school-room*, to accounts, and to the ordinary business transactions of life.

11. Much attention is now very properly paid to Penmanship in our schools. But it should be borne in mind that the great mass of the people employ this art chiefly for the purpose of recording business transactions and in business correspondence. How important, then, that correct forms and habits in these respects be early acquired! Pupils, it ought generally to be known, make the most rapid improvement in penmanship when engaged in writing something in which they are interested, and which they feel that they can after-

---

Quest. **9.** Is Book-keeping of more practical importance than many of the rules of arithmetic? — **10.** What application should be made of the principles of Grammar? — **11.** Is Penmanship of much practical importance? When will improvement in penmanship be most rapid?

ward turn to practical account. It cannot fail to be apparent, then, that independently of the benefits already enumerated, pupils will make greater improvement in this useful art by devoting a portion of their time to practical accounts than by writing after set copies.

12. It is but a few years since Book-keeping has been taught, to any considerable extent, in any grade of Schools in the country. And it is not even now taught in Colleges or Universities; nor is it embraced among the studies required to be pursued preparatory to admission to these institutions. As a consequence Graduates of Colleges and learned Professors are often less familiar with the simplest principles of business, than they are supposed to be with Latin and Greek roots, and with the orbits of the Planets and their Satellites! * Within the last few years Book-keeping *has* become a study in many of our Public Schools, in both cities and villages, and in the country. But Book-keeping by Double Entry is *not less attractive* as a Science, nor is it less important as a *means of discipline*, than are Geometry, Chemistry, and Natural Philosophy, or even Latin, Greek, and Astronomy. Add to this its practical importance, and absolute *necessity* in a commercial country, like ours, and the propriety of its introduction into our higher Seminaries of Learning generally must be apparent. Certain it is that no person can properly be regarded as *liberally educated* who is unacquainted with it.

13. The author of this treatise, in the execution of a plan laid many years ago, and practically tested in the school-room,

* A popular writer on education remarks that a teacher, who had kept a private school, was met in a country store by one of his patrons, who paid him for the tuition of his child, asking at the same time for a receipt. The teacher stared vacantly at his patron. "Just give me a bit of paper," said the patron, "to show you've got the money." "Oh, yes, sir," said the teacher; and taking a pen and paper, wrote the following: ☞ "I have got the money. J—— D——."

QUEST. **12.** How does Book-keeping rank, in point of importance, with branches commonly taught in schools? Is a knowledge of Book-keeping necessary to a liberal education?

has sought to supply what many practical teachers with whom he has compared views upon the subject in various portions of the country, have hitherto considered a *desideratum*. The study of this work may be advantageously commenced as soon as the pupil is familiar with the fundamental rules of arithmetic; and it may be successfully prosecuted in connection with any of the branches of an English education. The following are some of its distinguishing characteristics: *

1. Before introducing the pupil to accounts in which debit and credit entries occur, which is usually the first thing done in treatises on Book-keeping, a business transaction is defined, and the mode of entering the same in the books of both debtor and creditor illustrated. Several transactions are then stated, in various phraseology, and the entries to be made in the books of both parties further exemplified. These entries — which are in all cases made in *script* that closely resembles *writing* — afford good *models* for the learner. Then, in the first example of accounts that is presented, the transactions entered are on the same folio stated in common language, which enables the learner fully to comprehend the whole matter.

2. After giving a few specimens of the mode of keeping accounts by the first and simplest form, together with the necessary instructions to the learner, a series of *business transactions*, drawn from the ordinary pursuits of life, are introduced, in the form of *problems to be solved*. In their solution it becomes necessary, from inspecting the transactions, merely, to compute the value of whatever has been bought or sold, the price and the quantity being given; to make the requisite debit and credit entries, after first determining to which side of the account each transaction belongs; and then to balance the several accounts, which are to be

* Since the first publication of this work, in 1851, other volumes on the same subject have been printed, in which some of these distinguishing features have been copied; but in no other work, so far as the writer knows, can they all be found. New features of interest are also introduced into this revised edition.

written out like the patterns already set, and entered in a blank book prepared for that purpose.

3. Numerous Examples for Practice are likewise introduced in each of the five remaining forms of account, with accompanying blank Account Books appropriately ruled, in which they are to be entered when solved. These blank books contain engraved Forms for writing up Day Book, Journal, and Ledger, and for Notes, Drafts, and Bills of Exchange, with business forms generally, and may hence advantageously be employed as writing-books.

4. The instructions in relation to the mode of keeping accounts, which will be found sufficiently full for all ordinary purposes, even in the simplest forms, are generally given on the same page or folio with the illustrative examples, with carefully prepared questions for the examination of classes.

5. For the convenience of Teachers in examining the work of their classes, as well as for the encouragement of the private learner, a Key has been prepared to accompany this work, in which all the Examples for Practice are correctly entered in the various books used, and the accounts balanced and closed, so that no teacher, however inexperienced in keeping accounts, need shrink from undertaking to prepare himself for instructing classes in the use of this book.

6. The present *Revised Edition* of this work, while it retains the simplicity and gradually progressive character of former editions, is more complete than they were, and especially in Double Entry. The Diagram exhibiting the mode of closing accounts, p. 183, will enable the learner readily to comprehend what has hitherto been justly regarded as the most difficult feature of Double Entry Book-keeping.

7. The Examples for Practice, interspersed throughout the work, give the pupil the benefit of combining the Theory and Practice of accounts, and of deriving at once the advantages of both school-room and counting-room.

8. All the real advantages of *printing in colors* are incor-

porated into this edition, and still it is furnished at an unprecedentedly low price for a complete treatise on Book-keeping.

These characteristics are believed to be peculiar to this work. They make the whole subject perfectly intelligible to the intermediate classes in our common schools, as well as to those more advanced, and invest it with so much of interest as to render it highly attractive. In its use, it is confidently believed scholars will more rapidly acquire that facility in making business computations which is most desirable, than by devoting the same time exclusively to the study of arithmetic, as has hitherto been generally practiced; that they will make greater proficiency in penmanship than though an equal amount of time were devoted to writing after set copies; and that they will at the same time more readily acquire a thorough and practical knowledge of Book-keeping than from the study of any work that has heretofore been given to the public. So, view it in what light we may, the advantages arising from the study of Book-keeping, with the improved methods here presented, are too great and too numerous to allow much time to elapse before its general introduction into all our common, intermediate, and high schools.

Note. By referring to the opinions of Teachers who have used this book, and of Practical Educators who have carefully examined its claims, it will be seen that the views of the author, as here expressed, are regarded as fully realized by those who have given most attention to the subject, and are competent to judge.

PART FIRST.

GENERAL BOOK-KEEPING.

ART. **14.** BOOK-KEEPING is the art of keeping accounts in such a manner that a person may at any time know the true state of his business, or of his debts and credits, by an inspection of his books. The term General Book-keeping signifies that kind of book-keeping which is suitable for persons generally, such as farmers, mechanics, professional men, retailers, and, indeed, all persons except merchants engaged in a wholesale business.

15. Were persons universally to receive an equivalent for their wares when sold, and were they enabled to pay at the time for whatever they have occasion to purchase, it would still be desirable to keep a record of their business transactions. This necessity becomes imperative whenever products and goods are bought and sold without making payment at the time.

DEBTOR AND CREDITOR.

16. Whenever one person receives any thing from another, which he does not pay for at the time, he is said to *go in debt* for it, and is called a Debtor. A person who sells property without receiving his pay at the time, is said to *give credit* for it, and is called a Creditor. In other words, the *receiver* is always the Debtor, and the *giver* is always the Creditor. In keeping accounts it is customary, and more

QUEST. **14.** What is Book-keeping? What is meant by General Book-keeping? —**15.** Is it always desirable to keep a record of business transactions? When does this necessity become imperative?—**16.** When does a person become a Debtor? When a Creditor? When property exchanges hands without payment being made at the time, what general rule is stated in relation to the *receiver* and *giver* of it?

convenient, to abridge and write Dr. for Debtor, and Cr. for Creditor.

17. The act of buying or selling is called a Transaction. In every transaction there must be both a *buyer* and a *seller.* Where the property which exchanges hands is not paid for at the time of the transfer, the buyer becomes a Debtor, and the seller a Creditor. The following will serve as an illustration of the correct use of the terms already employed:

TRANSACTION.—James Armitage buys of Isaac Merrill one pair of Kip Boots, for which he is to pay him four dollars.

In this transaction James Armitage is the Debtor, because he is the *receiver;* and Isaac Merrill is the Creditor, because he is the *giver;* or, in other words, the furnisher.

The parties make the following entries in their respective books, under the date of the transaction:

Isaac Merrill writes in his book,

James Armitage, *Dr.*

To one Pair of Kip Boots, . . *$4.00*

James Armitage writes in his book,

Isaac Merrill, *Cr.*

By one Pair of Kip Boots, . . . *$4.00*

18. By examining these entries the pupil will see that the creditor writes the debtor's name in his book, and that the debtor writes the creditor's name in his book. This should be remembered, for it constitutes an invariable rule.

19. The word *To,* with which the creditor commences the entry in his book, indicates the passage of whatever has been sold, from him *to* the debtor; and the word *By,* with which the

QUEST. **16.** What abbreviations are used for Debtor and Creditor? — **17.** What is a Transaction? What must there be in every Transaction? Which becomes the Debtor, and which the Creditor? State a Transaction. In this Transaction who is the Debtor, and why? Who the Creditor, and why? In the Transaction stated, what entries should the parties make in their respective books? — **18.** Whose name does the creditor write in his book? Whose name does the debtor write in his book? Why ought this to be remembered? — **19.** What does the word *To*, with which the creditor commences the entry in his book, indicate? What the word *By*, with which the debtor commences the entry in his book?

debtor commences the entry in his book, the reception *by* him of that which the creditor has charged to him. In other words, the *To*, on the Dr. side of an account, indicates indebtedness *to* us from the person named in the account; and the *By*, on the Cr. side of the account, indicates indebtedness *by* us to the person named in the account.

20. The following examples will further illustrate the mode of entering transactions in the books of both debtor and creditor, with which the pupil should become familiar before progressing further. For this purpose separate sheets of paper may be used. Let the pupil write the transactions on one page, numbering them, and make the proper entries on another page, with their corresponding numbers and correct dates, as in the annexed examples. The *transactions* may be copied from the book. The *entries* should be made like those in the examples given: but they should be made from *an examination of the transaction;* not copied from the book. The pupil might also write out additional transactions, and having studied them carefully, be prepared in recitation to give the entries either on the blackboard, in writing, or orally, all of which methods might in turn be practiced.

21. The *price* and the *quantity* being given, the learner should, from the first, invariably compute the *value* of all articles bought or sold, whether the calculations are made in the book or not. It would be to his advantage to do this in studying any treatise on Book-keeping. But in the use of this work it becomes *absolutely necessary;* for the pupil will soon be called upon to record transactions where such computations are unavoidable.

QUEST. **20.** Should *entries* be copied from the book? How should they be made? —**21.** What computations should the learner invariably make? Are such computations *avoidable* in the study of this treatise?

State the first transaction, and give the entries to be made in the books of both parties. State the second transaction and the entries. The third, etc. Let the pupil state additional transactions, and give the entries orally, or on the blackboard.

SEVERAL TRANSACTIONS:

TRANSACTION 1. JANUARY 1st, 1860.

James Armitage buys of Isaac Merrill one pair of Kip boots, for which he is to pay him four dollars.

James Armitage is the debtor, because he is the receiver. Isaac Merrill is the creditor, because he is the giver.

TRANSACTION 2. JANUARY 2d, 1860.

Hallock & Raymond sell to John S. Barry one suit of clothes, for which he is to pay them fifty-two dollars.

John S. Barry is the debtor, because he is the receiver. Hallock & Raymond are the creditors, because they are the givers, or the sellers.

TRANSACTION 3. JANUARY 3d, 1860.

William H. Boyd sells to Charles G. Johnson 40 lbs. of nails, for six cents a pound.

C. G. Johnson is the debtor, because he is the receiver. Wm. H. Boyd is the creditor, because he is the giver.

TRANSACTION 4. JANUARY 4th, 1860.

Alex. McFarren buys of Harper & Brothers 4 dozen copies of Mayhew on Education, at $9.00 a dozen.

Alex. McFarren is the debtor, because he is the receiver. Harper & Brothers are the creditors, because they are the givers, or the sellers.

MODE OF ENTERING THEM.

1863.		Isaac Merrill writes in his book,			
Jan.	*1*	*James Armitage, ... Dr.*			
		To one Pair of Kip Boots,		*4*	*00*
		James Armitage writes in his book,			
Jan.	*1*	*Isaac Merrill, ... Cr.*			
		By one Pair of Kip Boots,		*4*	*00*

1860.		Hallock & Raymond write in their book,			
Jan.	*2*	*John S. Barry, ... Dr.*			
		To one Suit of Clothes, . .		*52*	*00*
		John S. Barry writes in his book,			
Jan.	*2*	*Hallock & Raymond, . . Cr.*			
		By one Suit of Clothes, . .		*52*	*00*

1860.		Wm. H. Boyd writes in his book,			
Jan.	*3*	*C. G. Johnson, ... Dr.*			
		To 40 lbs. of Nails, . .	*.06*	*2*	*40*
		C. G. Johnson writes in his book,			
Jan.	*3*	*Wm. H. Boyd, ... Cr.*			
		By 40 lbs. of Nails, . .	*.06*	*2*	*40*

1860.		Harper & Brothers write in their book,			
Jan.	*4*	*Alex. McFarren, ... Dr.*			
		To 4 doz. Mayhew on Ed'n,	*9.00*	*36*	*00*
		Alex. McFarren writes in his book,			
Jan.	*4*	*Harper & Brothers, . . . Cr.*			
		By 4 doz. Mayhew on Ed'n,	*9.00*	*36*	*00*

ACCOUNT BOOKS.

22. The number of books necessary for use, and the particular mode of keeping one's accounts, must depend upon the nature and extent of his business. Forms are sometimes given for Farmers; others, for Mechanics; and others still, for Merchants. But so great is the difference in the extent and variety of business carried on by these and other classes of persons, that some farmers find it desirable to keep a greater number of books than are requisite for mechanics; and other farmers, and mechanics, not unfrequently do a more varied and extensive business than is sometimes carried on by the merchant. In a treatise on General Book-keeping, then, it seems befitting to commence with the simplest form of accounts, which will be found convenient for persons engaged in a limited business of almost any kind, and afterward introduce others, and leave persons to select the form they shall deem best adapted to their particular business, taking into the account both its nature and extent.

23. Three forms for keeping accounts are presented, in this treatise, in Single Entry, and three in Double Entry.

FIRST FORM OF ACCOUNTS.

24. The LEDGER, which is indispensable, even where the Day Book and Journal are used as preliminary books, is the most important book in General Book-keeping, and the only one necessary in the first form of accounts. Its object is to show how the owner of the book stands toward the various persons with whom he has credit transactions.

QUEST. **22.** Upon what must the number of books used and the mode of keeping one's accounts depend? Why cannot particular forms be prescribed for Farmers, Mechanics, and Merchants? — **23.** How many forms for keeping accounts are given in this treatise? — **24.** What book only is necessary in the first form? Can the Ledger be dispensed with when the Day Book and Journal are used as preliminary books? What is the object of the Ledger?

25. Two pages opposite each other are appropriated for each individual account. The name of each person with whom we open an account (and his residence when this is necessary to identify him) should be written in a bold hand at the top of the page, or at the head of the account, for a title, as in the annexed examples.

26. The left-hand page is devoted to the Dr. entries of the account, and the right-hand page to the Cr. entries. It should be borne in mind that the word *To,* which commences each entry on the Dr. side of an account, indicates indebtedness *to* us, from the person whose name stands at the head of the account; and that the word *By,* which commences each entry on the Cr. side of an account, indicates indebtedness *by* us, to the person with whom we keep the account. (Art. 19.)

27. The words *To* and *By,* as signs of Dr. and Cr. entries, are sometimes omitted, in both Single and Double Entry; and the Dr. and Cr. sides of an account are often both kept on the same .page, though not in this form of accounts. But in every form of accounts *two sets of money columns* are required. The *left-hand set* is uniformly employed for Dr. entries, and the *right-hand set* for Cr. entries.

28. In the first form of accounts each page is divided by perpendicular lines into five spaces; in the first of which, commencing at the left-hand, the year and month are entered; in the second, the day of the month; in the third, the items bought or sold; and in the fourth and fifth, their value in dollars and cents.

QUEST. **25.** What space is appropriated to an account in the first form? What should be written at the head of each person's account? When should the *residence* of a person be given in the title of his account? — **26.** When two pages are appropriated to an account, which is devoted to the Dr. entries? Which to the Cr. entries? What is said of the words *To* and *By*? — **27.** Are these words ever omitted? How many sets of money columns are always required? How are they employed? — **28.** Into how many spaces is each page divided, and what should be entered in the several spaces?

29. When a person has occasion to use several Ledgers, as all do who engage extensively in business, it is customary to designate them by the letters of the alphabet, thus: Ledger A; Ledger B; etc. Different Ledgers are likewise frequently employed by persons at the same time, when engaged in an extended and varied business, separate Ledgers being devoted to retail sales, and to different branches of one's business. In such cases the results of these smaller Ledgers are periodically carried to the principal Ledger.

THE INDEX.

30. The Index is a small book in which the names of all persons having accounts in the Ledger, and the titles of accounts other than personal, are arranged in alphabetical order, under their initial letters, with reference to the folios or pages in which they stand. When small Ledgers are employed the Index may be conveniently written in a few of the first pages of the Ledger: but where large Ledgers are used, it will be found more convenient to employ a separate Index. When an account is transferred from one folio to another, as in the case of Henry Van Allen, both folios should be noted in the Index. This account, originally kept on the 8th folio, has been carried to the 9th.

QUEST. **29.** When a person has several Ledgers, how are they usually designated? When are different Ledgers employed at the same time? Where are the results of these Ledgers carried? — **30.** What is the Index? When may it be kept in the Ledger? When an account is transferred to a new folio what should be noted in the Index?

INDEX TO LEDGER A.

1 *James Brown* **Dr.**

1860.				$	cts.
Jan.	5	To 4 Cords Hickory . . .	1.75	7	00
"	10	" 10 Bbls. Apples . . .	1.25	12	50
Feb.	2	" 4 Tons Hay	6.50	26	00
Dec.	28	" Cash to Balance		12	00
				57	50

31. The above is an account with James Brown, a Blacksmith, in which seven transactions are entered.

Transaction 1. January 2d, 1860. James Brown shoes my horses, (each pupil may suppose them his,) for which I am to pay him $1.75. Here I am the receiver, and hence the debtor. James Brown is the giver, and hence the creditor. I, then, having written his name in my book, credit him with the amount of the work done for me; but as the last two columns are understood to be for dollars and cents, it was not necessary to write the sign for dollars and cents.

Tr. 2. Jan. 5th. I sell James Brown 4 cords of Hickory wood, for which he is to pay me $1.75 a cord. In this transaction he is the receiver, and hence the debtor, and I accordingly debit him for the amount, $7.00.

Tr. 3. Jan. 10th. I sell James Brown 10 bbls. of Apples at $1.25 a bbl., amounting in all to $12.50, and again debit him, as in the 2d transaction.

Tr. 4. Feb. 2d. I sell James Brown four tons of Hay at $6.50 a ton, amounting to $26.00, and debit him accordingly, he having been the receiver, and hence the debtor, in each of the last three transactions.

Tr. 5. June 3d. I buy of James Brown one Lumber Wagon, for which I am to pay him $50.00. Here he again

QUEST. **31.** How many transactions in the account with James Brown? What is the first transaction, and what the entry? What the second, and entry? The third, and entry? Fourth, and entry? Fifth, and entry?

James Brown Cr.

1860.			$	cts.
Jan.	2	By Shoeing Span of Horses . .	1	75
June	3	" 1 Lumber Wagon . . .	50	00
Nov.	10	" Repairing Sleigh . . .	4	50
"	15	" Shoeing Horse	1	25
			57	50

becomes the giver, or furnisher, and I the receiver. I hence credit him accordingly.

Tr. 6. Nov. 10th. James Brown repairs my Sleigh, for which he charges me $4.50. In this transaction, as in the last, he is the giver, and I am the receiver, and I hence credit him with the amount of the work done.

Tr. 7. Nov. 15th. Here James Brown shoes one of my horses, and the entry exhibits the necessary credit.

32. *Settlement.* Dec. 28th. Accounts should be settled at least once every year. As, then, the end of the year approaches, I call on James Brown for my annual settlement with him. We first add the sums in the money columns of the credit side of the account, and find they amount to $57.50, which is the sum total of all I have received from him. We next add the sums in the money columns of the debit side, and find they amount to $45.50, which is the sum total of all I have let him have. We then subtract the amount of the debits from the amount of the credits. This gives a remainder of $12.00, which is the amount of my indebtedness to him. I pay him this sum, and debit him "To Cash to Balance, $12.00." Finally, I draw single lines under the money columns, and after adding them and placing the amount, $57.50, under each, draw double lines beneath, to show that the account is balanced and closed.

QUEST. **31.** What the sixth transaction and entry? Seventh, and entry? — **32.** How often should accounts be settled? How is this account settled and closed?

2		Samuel Adams		Dr.
1860.			$	cts.
Jan.	10	To 75 Bush. Wheat 80	60	00
"	15	" 80 " Corn 40	32	00
Mar.	16	" 40 " Potatoes 35	14	00
			106	00
1861.				
Jan.	1	To Balance (due me) . .	8	17

33. The foregoing is an account with Samuel Adams, a Retail Merchant. I have sold him produce at three different times, amounting in all to $106.00. Dec. 31.—I call on him for settlement. By adding the sums credited to him, we find they amount to $97.83. By subtracting this sum from the amount of his debits, it appears there is due me $8.17. As I have no occasion to use either money or goods at this time, and expect to do my trading with him another year, the account is balanced as follows: I credit him "By Balance, $8.17." This done, the debits and credits amount to the same. I now draw single lines under the money columns, directly opposite each other, as before, placing the amount under them, and drawing the double lines beneath, to signify that the account has been examined and *found correct.* The $8.17 is entered in different type from the rest of the ac-

QUEST. **33.** How is the account with Samuel Adams settled? What of the balance?

Samuel Adams Cr.

1860.			$	cts.
Jan.	4	By 25 lbs. Loaf Sugar . .13	3	25
"	10	" 2¼ Yds. Broadcloth . . 4.00	9	00
"	"	" 2¾ " Cassimere . . 2.00	5	50
"	"	" Trimmings for Coat and Vest	2	75
Feb.	4	" 21 Yds. Sheeting 11	2	31
"	"	" 1 lb. Black Tea . . .		75
Apr.	12	" Bill of Crockery . . .	12	70
"	"	" 30 Grain Bags 25	7	50
"	"	" Bill of Goods for John Bruce	25	75
July	2	" my Order to John Bruce	22	50
Nov.	8	" 1 Piece of Calico, 34 Yds. .15	5	10
Dec.	14	" 8 lbs. Brown Sugar . .09		72
"	31	" Balance (due me) . . .	8	17
			106	00

count. This indicates that it is *due me*, but *not paid.* Such entries are often made in *red ink.* The Balance I debit him below, as the amount due me on settlement.

34. When one side of the account contains more entries than the other, as in this example, an oblique line should be drawn across the unoccupied space, as is here done. The Dr. and Cr. amounts, when footed, should equal each other, and be on the same *horizontal* line, as in this example.

35. The Bill of Goods on account of John Bruce, my hired man, bought April 12, I credit to the Merchant and debit to Bruce; also my Order in his favor of July 2. When goods are credited "by bill," as in this instance, the bill should be kept till the accounts are settled.

QUEST. **34.** When one side of the account contains more entries than the other, what rule should be observed in relation to the footings?—**35.** What items that are credited in this account are debited in another account? When goods are credited by bill, how long should the bills be kept?

John Bruce Dr.

1860.			$	cts.
Apr.	12	To Bill of Goods from Sam. Adams	25	75
"	17	" W. Wood for Making Clothes	7	50
July	2	" my Order on Samuel Adams	22	50
Sept.	12	" my Note at 60 Days to Balance	29	25
			85	00

36. Here is represented an account with John Bruce, my hired man: (for the terms of my contract with him, see Memorandum Book, 58th page.) The first and third *debits* in his account are *credits* in the account with Samuel Adams, as exhibited on the last preceding page. I have also debited him the amount paid W. Wood on his behalf for making a suit of clothes, and with my Note to balance, and thus closed the account. I have debited him with my Note, the same as I should have done with Cash, had I paid him the money to balance. This fulfills my agreement with him, as per memorandum referred to. My note I shall of course expect to pay when it becomes due. (See Bills Payable, 50th page.)

37. These entries, and the two referred to in the account with Samuel Adams, are made in accordance with a principle already stated and elucidated, which enables us to determine where to enter every transaction belonging to personal accounts. The principle is this: The *receiver* is always the Debtor, and the *giver* is always the Creditor. No distinction is made between cash, notes, goods, accepted orders, (see remarks in relation to Orders, Art. 164,) money due for services, or houses and lands. Whenever a person *receives* any

QUEST. **36.** In case I make an order on Samuel Adams for $22.50, payable to John Bruce, how should I enter the transaction in their respective accounts? In case I give my note to John Bruce to balance an account on settlement, how do I enter the transaction in his account?

John Bruce Cr. 3

1860.			$	cts.
Apr.	12	By 3 Months' Labor . . 10.00	30	00
Sept.	12	" 5 do. do. . . . 11.00	55	00
			85	00

of these or other property from you, or you pay them *on his behalf*, the transaction should be entered on the Dr. side of his account. When he pays them to you, or on your behalf, and thus becomes the *giver*, and you the receiver, the transaction should be entered on the Cr. side of his account. In the case of my order on Samuel Adams for $22.50 in favor of John Bruce, Adams is the *giver* to Bruce, on my account, and hence my Creditor; and Bruce is the *receiver* from Adams, on my account, and hence my Debtor. This principle is of universal application.

38. The symbol of a Pair of Scales on the Title Page, which beautifully illustrates the general principle that the Dr. and Cr. sides of an account ought always to balance, particularly illustrates the account here introduced. As the four smaller weights at the left arm of the scales are exactly counterpoised by the two larger ones at the right arm, so the four smaller entries on the Dr. side of the account exactly balance the two larger ones on the Cr. side. Another symbol is referred to in Art. 277.

QUEST. **37.** What general rule is stated which enables us to determine on which side of an account to enter a transaction? Does the rule apply to notes and orders as well as to money and goods? When a person receives property from you, or you pay it on his behalf, how is the transaction entered? How, when he pays to you or on your behalf? Is this principle of universal application? — **38.** What principle does the symbol on the title page illustrate? Apply that symbol to this account.

4 **Wheatfield, 18 Acres Dr.**

			$	cts.
1859.				
June	10	To 12 Days Plowing . . 2.00	24	00
"	20	4 do. Harrowing . . 1.50	6	00
Aug.	28	" 10 do. Plowing . . 2.00	20	00
Sept.	10	" 27 Bush. Seed Wheat . .80	21	60
"	"	" 2 Days Sowing . . 1.00	2	00
"	"	" 8 do. Harrowing . . 1.50	12	00
1860.				
July	10	" Harvesting 18 Acres . . 1.50	27	00
Oct.	1	" Threshing 316 Bushels Wheat	22	20
"	13	" Marketing do. do. do.	6	00
"	"	" Interest at $20 per Acre . .07	25	20
"	"	" Profit on the Crop	70	20
			236	20

39. The above is an account with a Wheatfield of 18 acres, from which it appears that the net profit (after paying the interest on the value of the land, and all the expenses of raising the crop) is seventy dollars and twenty cents. The account is kept just as an account with a person is: The field is *debited* with every thing put upon it, with every expense made on its account, and with the interest on the land at a fair valuation. It is *credited* with every thing it produces, and with every thing received on its account. The excess of the credits over the debits gives the net profit, which must be entered on the Dr. side of the account in order to balance. (Art. 33.) Accounts may be kept in like manner with every branch of one's business, whether agricultural, mechanical, commercial, or speculative.

Quest. 39. In the account with a Wheatfield of 18 acres, what is the net profit? How is the account kept? With what is the field debited, and with what credited? How is the net profit ascertained? With what kinds of business may accounts be kept in this way?

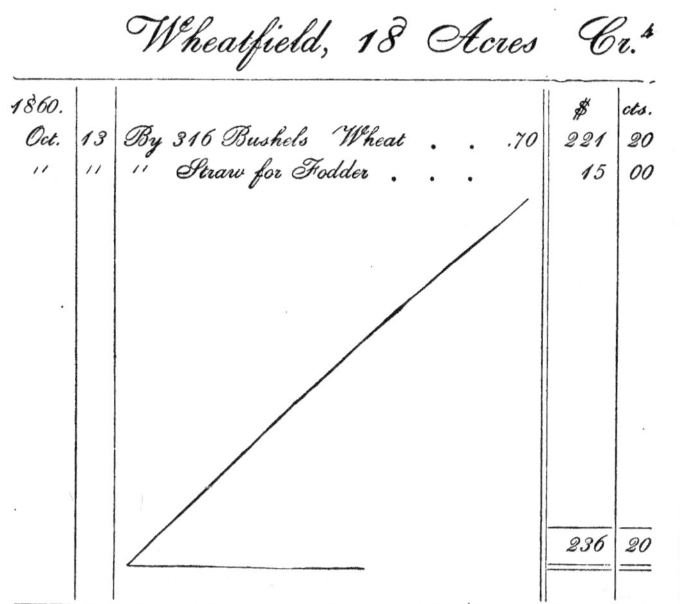

Wheatfield, 18 Acres Cr.

1860.				$	cts.
Oct.	13	By 316 Bushels Wheat . .	.70	221	20
"	"	" Straw for Fodder . . .		15	00
				236	20

40. Were persons generally to keep such accounts, they could ascertain, with great accuracy, what pursuits afford certain profits, and what particular department of their business is most lucrative; also, what enterprises are hazardous and unproductive; and, by regulating themselves accordingly, they would of course best promote their own pecuniary interests, and at the same time contribute most effectually to advance the general prosperity of the community in which they live. (Arts. 218 to 225.)

41. When the debits in such an account exceed the credits, and it becomes necessary in balancing the account to make the last entry on the Cr. side, it is evident the enterprise is attended with *loss*, as is exemplified in the account with a Grain Speculator on the next folio.

QUEST. **40.** What advantages would result to the individual and to the community if persons generally were to keep such accounts? — **41.** When the debits in such an account exceed the credits, is the enterprise attended with *gain* or *loss?*

5		Wheat Account		Dr.
1859.			$	cts.
Nov.	10	To Cash for 10,000 Bush. Wheat .72	7200	00
"	"	" Charges to Monroe per Bu. .15	1500	00
1860.				
Apr.	20	" Charges at Monroe do. .04	400	00
"	"	" Insurance against Fire ½ per cent.	43	50
"	27	" Lake Freight to Buffalo .03	300	00
"	"	" Marine Insurance ½ per cent.	43	50
May	10	" Com. for Selling at Buffalo .01	100	00
"	"	" Exchange on $8700 at ½ per cent.	43	50
"	"	" Interest on same for 6 mos. .07	304	50
			9935	00

42. Above is the account of a Grain Speculator, who made a purchase in Southern Michigan, the 10th of Nov., with the expectation of getting the same forward to Buffalo, making sales at 97 cents, and getting returns in two weeks. Had he realized his expectations he would have reduced the cost of the wheat to him in Buffalo, one cent per bushel of the charges in Monroe on account of storage for the winter,

1859.				
Nov.	10	To Cash for 10.000 Bush. Wheat .72	7200	00
"	"	" Charges to Monroe per Bu. .15	1500	00
"	24	" do. at do. do. .03	300	00
"	"	" Lake Freight and Marine Ins.	343	50
"	"	" Commission and Exchange . .	143	50
"	"	" Interest on $8700 for ½ month .07	25	37
"	"	" Amount to Balance (Gain) . . .	**187**	**63**
			9700	00

QUEST. **42.** — What was lost by a Grain Speculator in the Wheat Account here given?

Wheat Account *Cr.* 5

			$	cts.
1860.				
May	5	*By Proceeds of 4000 Bu. Wheat .87½*	3500	00
"	10	" *do. 6000 do. .87*	5220	00
"	"	" Amount to Balance (Loss) .	1215	00
			9935	00

the insurance against fire, and 5½ months interest—amounting in all to $422.63
And his receipts would have been greater by . 980.00
Making an actual difference in the result of . . $1402.63
Hoping to *gain* $187.63, as appears from his figuring below, before engaging in the enterprise, he actually *lost* $1215.00, as appears from the account as given above.

1859.				
Nov.	25	*By Returns on 10,000 Bu. Wheat .97*	9700	00
		Note. In order to exhibit this account complete on one folio, the Lake Freight and Marine Insurance in the opposite entries (which are the same as in the above account) are combined; also the charges for Commission and Exchange.		
			9700	00

Quest. 42. What had he hoped to gain? What difference, and how made up?

Cornfield, 8 Acres Dr.

				$	cts.
1859.					
Apr.	20	To ¼ of 56 Loads Manure	.25	3	50
May	1	" 3 Days Plowing	2.00	6	00
"	2	" 1 do. Harrowing		1	50
"	3	" 1½ do. Marking-out	1.50	2	25
"	5	" 1¼ Bu. Seed Corn	.50		63
"	"	" 4 Days Planting	.75	3	00
"	20	" 2 do. Cultivating	1.50	3	00
June	1	" 2 do. do.	1.50	3	00
"	15	" 2 do. Plowing	1.50	3	00
Sept.	10	" 5⅓ do. Cutting and Shocking	.75	4	00
Oct.	10	" Husking and Binding Stalks		20	00
"	"	" Putting into Cribs		8	00
1860.					
Feb.	1	" Threshing 800 Bu. Corn	.01½	12	00
"	15	" Marketing do. do.	.01½	12	00
"	"	" Interest at $20 per Acre	.07	11	20
"	"	" Profit on the Crop		255	92
				349	00

43. The profit on this crop of Corn is very great, as is shown by the last entry on the Dr. side of the account; but then, the soil that produced it was very fruitful, and required but a small amount of labor in cultivation. Corn, moreover, usually requires twice hoeing; but this, which was raised on the River Raisin, in Monroe county, Michigan, was not hoed at all. It was "cultivated" between the rows, in one direction, the 20th of May, and in the other direction the

QUEST. **43.** Here is presented an account with a crop of corn of eight acres. What is the profit on the crop? How are this large yield and consequent profit accounted for? How was the field cultivated?

Cornfield, 8 Acres Cr.[6]

			$	cts.
1859.				
Oct.	10	By 10 Loads of Stalks, . . . 1.50	15	00
"		" 14 do. do. for Fodder 1.00	14	00
1860.				
Feb.	15	" 800 Bushels Corn 40	320	00
			349	00

1st of June; and it was plowed out once only, without hoeing, on the 15th day of the latter month. This mode of culture, and this yield, are common in the new States.

44. This crop was debited with only *one-fourth* the expense of manuring, because the land was permanently enriched, and the benefit will probably be realized in the next three crops to as great an extent as in this. It is hence apparent that but one-fourth of the expense of enriching should be debited to this crop.

QUEST. 44. Why was not this crop debited with the whole expense of enriching?

7		Cash			Dr.
1860.				$	cts.
Jan.	1	To Cash on hand		14	50
"	4	" 4 Cords Wood	1.50	6	00
"	10	" 10 bbls. Apples . . .	2.00	20	00
"	15	" 14 Cords Wood . . .	1.50	21	00
"	23	" 2 bbls. Pork	9.00	18	00
				79	50
Feb.	1	To Balance brought down . .		38	67

45. An account may and should be kept with Cash, the same as with an individual, as in the above example. Persons who have a limited cash deal may keep their Cash Account in the Ledger, and in the same manner they do their personal accounts. But when one's cash account is extensive, or the entries in it become frequent and numerous, it will be best to keep the account in a separate Cash Book provided for that purpose, which should be balanced at the close of each day. In opening the account, Cash should be debited with the amount on hand. All moneys *received* should be entered on the Dr. side of the Cash account, and all moneys *paid out*, on the Cr. side of the account. In balancing the account, Cash should be credited with the amount on hand. But as this amount is *not* paid out, it is here entered in different type, and usually in *red ink*, to denote that fact. Cash is then debited for the balance.

46. The amount on hand at the opening of an account with Cash, together with the sums *received* at different times,

QUEST. **45.** How may an account be kept with Cash? When may the Cash account be kept in the Ledger? When should a separate Cash Book be provided? With what should Cash be debited on opening the account? What entries are made on the Dr. and what on the Cr. side of the account? What credit should be made in balancing the account? Why is this entry made in different type?—**46.** What amounts should be equal? What do the Dr. and what the Cr. entries show?

Cash *Cr.*

1860.				$	cts.
Jan.	3	*By 1 Pr. Buckskin Mittens* . .			63
"	7	" *10 lbs. Brown Sugar* . .	.07		70
"	10	" *Books as per Bill* . . .		7	50
"	17	" *Subscription for Preaching* .		18	00
"	24	" *1 Qr's Tuition for 2 Sch's*	7.00	14	00
"	31	" Balance on hand		38	67
				79	50

should exactly equal the amount of the sums *paid out* and the cash on hand at the time of balancing the account. The Dr. entries show what Cash has been *received* for, and the Cr. entries show what Cash has been *paid* for.

47. The first entry in the Cash account must always be on the Dr. side; for no person can pay out money unless he first has it on hand. It is likewise apparent that the credit entries in the Cash account can never exceed the amount of the debit entries. When these are exactly equal, there can be no Cash on hand. When the Dr. side of the account amounts to more than the Cr. side, the difference, if the account has been correctly kept, will exactly equal the Cash on hand.

48. An account may be balanced and continued on the same page, or two accounts may be kept on the same folio, as in the following examples, according to circumstances. Whenever a folio is filled, and the account not closed, the two sides of the account should be added and the amount carried to some other folio designated. (See example on the next folio.)

Quest. 47. Where must the first entry be made in the Cash Account? Why? Can the credit entries ever exceed the debit entries? When the Dr. side amounts to more than the Cr. side, what should the difference be equal to? — **48.** When an account is settled, may it be reopened on the same page? May two accounts be kept on the same folio? When a folio is filled and the account not closed, what should be done?

8

John Martin Dr.

1859.				$	cts.
Jan.	10	To 10 lbs. Butter	.15	1	50
Feb.	4	" 12 " do.	.15	1	80
"	"	" 15 Bu. Corn	.40	6	00
July	2	" 20 Yds. Tow Cloth . .	.34	6	80
Nov.	30	" 40 Bushels Wheat . .	.80	32	00
Dec.	31	" Balance to new acct. . . .		4	72
				52	82

1860.					
Jan.	10	To 8 Bushels Potatoes . . .	.40	3	20
Apr.	4	" 6 " do. . . .	.44	2	64
Nov.	25	" 80 " Wheat . . .	.78	62	40
"	26	" 45 " Corn . . .	.35	15	75
				83	99

Henry Van Allen Dr.

1860.					
Jan.	6	To 2¼ Yds. Broadcloth for self	4.00	9	00
"	"	" 2½ Yds. Cassimere for Pants	2.30	5	75
"	"	" Trimmings for Suit Clothes		4	25
Feb.	4	" 40 lbs. Brown Sugar per Wife	.08	3	20
"	"	" 1 Piece Sheeting, 30½ Yds.	10	3	05
"	"	" 10 Yds. M. De Laine .	.34	3	40
"	"	" Trimmings			31
Apr.	9	" 4 Yds. Irish Linen . .	.56	2	24
"		" 1½ " Linen Edging . .	.20		30
				31	50

Amount to folio 9

John Martin Cr. 8

				$	cts.
1859.					
Jan.	10	By 6 lbs. Brown Sugar . .	.08		48
Feb.	4	" 10 Yds. Calico, by Julia .	.17	1	70
"	"	" Bill of Crockery . . .		6	50
July	2	" Cash advanced on Wheat .		40	00
"	"	" 1 Piece of Sheeting, 31 Yds.	.10	3	10
Nov.	30	" 10 lbs. Nails, by John .	.06		60
"	"	" 1 Currycomb, do. .			44
				52	82
1860.					
Jan.	1	By Balance brought down . .		4	72
Apr.	4	" 1 Piece Shirting, 32 Yds.	.09	2	88
May	1	" 2 Hoes for John and George	.88	1	76
Dec.	26	" Cash to Balance . . .		74	63
				83	99

Henry Van Allen Cr.

				$	cts.
1860.					
Jan.	10	By 20 Bushels of Wheat . .	.75	15	00
				15	00

See this account at the 73d page, kept by the *Second Form*.

Amount to folio 9

9 *Henry Van Allen* Dr.

1860.				$	cts.
May	10	To Amount from folio 8 . .		31	50
"	"	" 2 Linen Hdkfs. per Jane	37½		75
"	"	" 16 Yds. Watered Silk .	1.25	20	00
"	"	" 1 Pr. Kid Buskins . .		1	25
July	1	" Piece Shirting, 30 Yds. .	.11	3	30
"	"	" 14 lbs. Loaf Sugar . .	.14	1	96
Aug.	4	" 2 Palm Leaf Hats . . .	.31¼		63
"	10	" 10 Yds. Brown Linen .	.35	3	50
"	"	" 24 " Linen Gingham	.31	7	44
Oct.	12	" 4 " Broadcloth . .	3.00	12	00
"	"	" 1⅙ Doz. Buttons . . .	.25		29
"	"	" Trimmings per Bill . .		12	25
				94	87

49. This account is here continued from the preceding folio. It might have been carried to any other, as well as brought here, by making the proper entry at the foot of the page from which it is brought, showing the folio upon which it is continued.

50. The books of the Creditor should specify every item sold. This is always important, and especially so when the entries are of considerable amount. The last entry on the Dr. side of this account with H. Van Allen is hence *radically defective*, not a single article debited being specified. The Bill, if purchased by any other person than himself, may never reach him; or if it does, it may be mislaid, and in the settlement it may be impossible to satisfy him that this amount has ever been received by him, or on his account. The Debtor may *give credit* for goods as per bill received, if he choose to do so, as in the case of a "Bill of Crockery" in

QUEST. **50.** What should the books of the Creditor specify? What of the last Dr. entry in the account with H. Van Allen? May the Debtor give credit in his books per bill received? In such cases what should be done with the bill?

Henry Van Allen Cr.

1860.				$	cts.
May	10	By Amount from folio 8 . .		15	00
Oct.	15	" 90 Bushels Wheat . .	.87	78	30
Dec.	29	" Cash to Balance . . .		1	57
				94	87

See this account at the 73d page, kept by the *Second Form*.

the account with John Martin on the last folio, and as is twice done in the account with Samuel Adams—once for a "Bill of Crockery," and once for a "Bill of Goods for John Bruce." But even in such cases, to prevent any occasion for difficulty, it is better to preserve bills until the accounts are settled.

51. If on the Dr. side of my account with a person, I enter "To Bill of Goods," and carry out only the amount, he may not give me any credit at all, and on settlement he may dispute the account, and I may then be unable to specify a single article sold him. On the contrary, if I enter on the Cr. side of my account with a person, "By Bill of Goods," and give the amount, I thereby acknowledge the receipt of the *amount;* but in case the books do not exactly agree, difficulties may still arise in the settlement, if the bill is not preserved so as to compare items. The following rule should be observed for Dr. and Cr. entries:

QUEST. **51.** Why should the items sold be specified in the books of the Creditor, when they may be entered per bill in the books of the Debtor?

RULE FOR DR. AND CR. ENTRIES.

52. The Books of the Creditor should specify both the quantity and the value of every article sold. The Books of the Debtor should likewise specify both the quantity and the value of every article bought by him, unless *bills* are received of goods purchased, *which is always preferable.* When bills are given, the holder of them may enter the *amount only* in his account, but he should keep the bills on file until settlement.

BILLS OF PARCELS.

53. A BILL OF PARCELS is a statement of goods bought or sold at one time, embracing both the quantity and the price of each article, and the amount of the whole. If paid at the time of purchase, it should be receipted by the seller, as in the first example on the opposite page; if paid "by note," as in the second example; and if "charged in account," it should be entered as in the third example.

54. In case goods are paid for in money when purchased, it is sufficient for each party to enter the transaction in his Cash account. But even then, if there is a personal account between the parties, the merchant should debit the purchaser for the goods sold, and credit him for the money received.

55. When payment is made "by note," the merchant should make the necessary entry under the head of Bills Receivable, and the purchaser under the head of Bills Payable; and in case there is an account between the parties the whole transaction should be shown. (Art. 54.) But

56. When a bill of goods is "charged in account," the merchant should simply debit the purchaser with the items sold, which should be credited in the books of the latter.

QUEST. **52.** What rule is given for making Dr. and Cr. entries? — **53.** What is a bill of parcels? — **54.** When goods are paid for at the time of purchase, what entries should be made in the books of each party? — **55.** When payment is made "by note," what entries should be made? — **56.** When a bill of goods is "charged in account," what entries should the parties make in their books?

(1) *Detroit, July 10, 1860.*

James Henry,

Bought of C. G. Johnson,

24 Seamless Bags, at	.31	7.44
20 lbs. of Brown Sugar	.07	1.40
14 " Rice	.05	.70
1 " Black Tea		.75
Received Payment,		$10.29

Goods delivered to hired man.

C. G. Johnson,
Per C. Luce.

(2) *Chicago, August 12, 1860.*

Henry Hubbard,

Bought of Isaac Merrill,

1 Pair of Pegged Kip Boots	3.75
1 " Kid Buskins, for Wife	1.25
1 " " " for Daughter	1.00
Rec'd Payment by Note at 30 days,	$6.00

Isaac Merrill.

(3) *Boston, September 10, 1860.*

David Bronson,

Bought of Miller & Son,

10 lbs. Brown Sugar	.08	.80
16 Yds. Calico	.20	3.20
Charged in Account,		$4.00

ACCOUNTS CURRENT.

57. An ACCOUNT CURRENT is a record of the unsettled transactions between the parties named in the account, comprising both debits and credits. It should contain a list of the items bought and sold, together with their prices, and should show the date of each transaction; thus:

George Graham,
In Acct. with James Armitage, Dr.

1860.						
Jan.	*10*	*To 3 Gallons Molasses .50*	*1*	*50*		
"	*"*	*" 2 Sets Cups and Saucers*		*50*		
Feb.	*4*	*" 15 Yds. Calico . .15*	*2*	*25*		
"	*"*	*" 2½ " Flannel . .20*		*50*		
"	*"*	*" 3 Papers of Pins . .10*		*30*		
May	*10*	*" 4 lbs. Coffee . . .13*		*52*		
"	*"*	*" 12 lbs. Brown Sugar .09*	*1*	*08*	*$6*	*65*
		Cr.				
1860.						
Feb.	*4*	*By 10 lbs. Butter . .14*	*1*	*40*		
May	*10*	*" Cash per son George*	*1*	*60*		
		Balance due me . (Art. 33.)	3	65	*$6*	*65*

EXAMPLES FOR PRACTICE.

58. In the following examples, where several articles of the same kind are bought or sold, the price and the quantity are given, and the pupil is left to carry out the amount, which should uniformly be done. If the computations are correctly made, the accounts will exactly balance.

QUEST. 57. What is an account current? What should it contain and show?

James Farmer,
In Acct. with Ira Merchant, *Dr.*

1860.						
Jan.	10	To 3½ Yds. Flannel .50	---	---		
"	"	" 6 do. Calico . .15	---	---		
"	"	" 7¾ do. Shirting .16	---	---		
May	4	" 1 Hoe, per son John	---	88		
June	10	" 2 Scythes and Snaths	3	50	8	27
1860.		*Cr.*				
Jan.	10	By 9 Bushels Oats . .23	---	---		
May	4	" 4 Doz. Hens' Eggs .09	---	---		
June	16	" 8 do. do. . .08	---	---		
July	1	" Cash to Balance .	5	20	8	27

Isaac Paywell,
In Acct. with Ira Merchant, *Cr.*

1860.						
Feb.	12	By 40 Bushels Oats .27	---	---		
"	"	" 12 do. Corn .44	---	---		
"	15	" 60 do. Wheat .84	---	---	66	48
1860.		*Dr.*				
Mar.	10	To 4 Yds. Broadcloth 4.50	---	---		
"	"	" 16 do. Black Silk 1.00	---	---		
"	"	" Cash to Balance .	32	48	66	48

59. In the last example, the credits occurring before and exceeding the debits are placed first in the acct. Both examples are differently arranged under the Second Form of Accts.

Notes and Bills

No.	Date.		Maker's Name.	Indorser's Name.
	1860.			
1	May	10	Samuel Ware	H. Paywell
2	July	2	John N. Isham	None
3	Aug.	12	Thomas Payne	Timothy Trusty
4	Sept.	10	A. H. Murray	do. do.
5	"	20	James Darrow	H. Paywell

Notes and Bills

No.	Date.		Payee's Name.	Indorser's Name.
	1860.			
1	Sept.	12	John Bruce	None
	1861.			
2	June	10	John Owen	James Henry
3	July	1	do. do.	None
4	"	15	Grace Goodman	None

60. The term BILLS RECEIVABLE includes all written obligations for the payment of money which you hold against other persons, such as Promissory Notes, Due Bills, Orders, Drafts, etc. When any of these are received by you, they should be at once entered under the head, Bills Receivable, noting particulars, after which they may be placed on their proper files. Then, by referring to the Bill Book, it will be easy to see when any obligation you hold against another becomes due, where it is payable, etc. You thus save yourself the trouble of examining various packages of papers, the contents of which are here noted. Bills, when thus entered, may be readily referred to by number. Persons engaged in extensive business find it convenient to keep separate Bill Books; but those who transact a limited business may require only a folio of their Ledger, properly ruled.

QUEST. **60.** What are Bills Receivable? Where should they be entered when received, and why? What, then, can be ascertained by referring to the Bill Book?

Receivable.

Where Payable.	When Due.		Amount.		Remarks.
	1861.				
State Bank	May	29	75	50	Paid at Maturity
My Store	June	15	24	75	Pd. June 14, 1861
State Bank	"	21	60	00	Pd. June 21, 1861
Boston	Nov.	20	17	14	Pd. $10 July 10th
My Store	Dec.	30	25	00	

Payable.

Where Payable.	When Due.		Amount.		Remarks.
	1860.				
My House	Nov.	12	29	25	Paid at Maturity
	1861.				
Owen's Office	June	25	10	50	Pd. June 20, 1861
do. do.	July	15	20	00	Paid at Maturity
My House	Nov.	15	40	84	

61. The term BILLS PAYABLE includes all written obligations for the payment of money, of whatever kind, given by you to other persons. Whenever you give such an obligation you should enter the particulars in the Bill Book. It is of the utmost importance to note, at the time, at least the *amount* and *when due*, together with the *payee's name* and *where payable.*

62. The *maker* of a note (called also the giver or drawer) is the person who gives the note, and who must sign it. The *payee* of a note is the person to whom it is made payable. The place where a note is payable should always be specified whenever the *payee* (or holder of the note at the time it becomes due) does not expect to call at the *maker's* place of business, or at his residence for payment. (For other particulars pertaining to Bills, see Arts. 159 to 171.)

QUEST. **61.** What are Bills Payable? Where should they be entered when given? What should be especially noted? — **62.** Who is the *maker* of a note? Who the *payee?* When should the place where a note is payable be specified?

Bills Receivable Dr.

1860.				
May	10	No. 1, of Samuel Ware . . .	$75	50
July	2	No. 2, " Jno. N. Isham . .	24	75
Aug.	12	No. 3, " Thomas Payne . .	60	00
Sept.	10	No. 4, " A. H. Murray . .	17	14
"	20	No. 5, " James Darrow . .	25	00
			202	39
Dec.	1	To Balance brought down . . .	32	14

Bills Payable Dr.

1860.				
Nov.	12	Cash to John Bruce . . No. 1	$29	25
1861.				
June	20	Cash to Jno. Owen . . No. 2	10	50
July	15	do. " do. do. . . No. 3	20	00
Sept.	1	Balance (not due)	40	84
			100	59

63. In connection with the general statement concerning Bills Receivable and Bills Payable, presented on the last folio, it will be found convenient to keep a Dr. and Cr. account with each. This is done in the same manner that an account is kept with an individual, or with Cash.

64. When we *give* any thing for a Bill, or on its account, we *debit* it. When we *receive* any thing for a Bill, or on its account, we *credit* it. The first entry to every Bill Receivable is on the Dr. side of the account. The first entry to every Bill Payable is on the Cr. side of the account.

QUEST. **63.** How may a Dr. and Cr. account be kept with Bills Receivable and Bills Payable? — **64.** When do we *debit* a Bill, and when *credit* it? Where is the *first* entry to Bills Receivable, and where to Bills Payable?

Bills Receivable Cr.

1861.				
May	29	Cash of Samuel Ware . No. 1	$ 75	50
June	14	do. " J. N. Isham . No. 2	24	75
"	21	do. " T. Payne . . . No. 3	60	00
July	10	do. " A. H. Murray on No. 4	10	00
Dec.	1	Balance (unpaid)	32	14
			202	39

Bills Payable Cr.

1860.				
Sept.	12	No. 1, to John Bruce (Art. 36.)	$ 29	25
1861.				
June	10	No. 2, " Jno. Owen	10	50
July	1	No. 3, " do. do.	20	00
"	15	No. 4, " Grace Goodman . .	40	84
			100	59
Sept.	1	By Balance brought down . . .	40	84

65. The account exhibited on this folio is based upon transactions recorded upon the preceding folio. The entry made in each, under date Sept. 12, 1860, relates to a note given to John Bruce in the settlement of our personal account.

66. A person keeping a Dr. and Cr. account with Bills Receivable and Bills Payable, can, by periodically balancing these accounts, ascertain what amount remains unpaid on the obligations *he holds against others*, and whether this sum is increasing or lessening from time to time; also, *his own indebtedness* on account of notes and other bills payable, and whether it is increasing or diminishing in amount.

QUEST. **65.** Upon what transactions is the account here presented based? — **66.** What can a person keeping such an account at any time ascertain?

GENERAL SETTLEMENT.

67. A General Settlement shows how a person stands with the world, or with all persons with whom he transacts business, taken collectively. It is made by taking an inventory of one's property, to the fair value of which he must add the *sum of the balances due him* from others in the settlement of his *personal accounts,* and the balance due him on *bills receivable.* From the total amount of these he must deduct the *sum of the balances due others* in the settlement of his personal accounts, together with the balance that may become due from him on *bills payable.* The difference of these amounts will evidently represent his exact standing with all persons with whom he has business relations.

68. Such general settlements should be made at the end of each year, immediately after one's annual settlements take place. By comparing the result of each general settlement with those of preceding ones, persons can readily see how much they have gained or lost during the past year, or in any given number of years. But without such a general settlement it is impossible for persons engaged in an extensive debit and credit business to possess any definite knowledge of their exact standing with the world.

69. No one who has any adequate regard for his own pecuniary interests, and for his reputation as a business man, should fail to make such a settlement at the close of every year's business. In the light of such facts as would thus be thrown upon one's business, ultimate success is almost certain; while, if left to grope his way as it were in the dark, he not only jeopards success, but seems even to court a failure.

QUEST. **67.** What does a General Settlement show? How is a General Settlement made? — **68.** When should such a settlement be made? How can persons ascertain what they have gained or lost during the past year, or in any number of years? Can persons possess any definite knowledge of their standing with the world without such general settlements? — **69.** What is said of such settlements in connection with one's *success* or *failure* in business?

70. When a person's indebtedness exceeds what he possesses and what is due him, taken together, he is insolvent, and is sometimes said to be *worse than nothing.*

MEMORANDUM BOOK.

71. This book, whose name indicates its general character, is second in importance to the Ledger only. In it should be entered every thing of importance relating to a person's business that does not properly belong to the Ledger. It will often contain agreements, the carrying out of which will require frequent entries in the Ledger, as is illustrated in the case of John Bruce, whose account has already been given at pp. 32d and 33d. A memorandum of my agreement with him is given in the following Memorandum Book, under date Jan. 12th, 1860.

72. The Memorandum Book should commence with a general inventory of one's property. It should contain memorandums of agreements and of contracts of various kinds. It should not only contain a general statement of one's business affairs, but in it every important particular relating to his business which he ought himself to remember, or which should be known to his legal representatives, should be carefully recorded.

73. All business engagements of importance which you make, to be fulfilled hereafter, should be carefully recorded in this book at the time they are entered into; and when they are met, a brief entry should be made in the space left at the right, stating the facts. Where the engagement is simple, as in the case of my contract with Dr. J. Goodman, made March 16th, and promptly fulfilled, it is not necessary

QUEST. **70.** When is a person said to be *worse than nothing?* — **71.** What is said of the importance of the Memorandum Book? What should be entered in it? — **72.** With what should this book commence, and what should it contain? — **73.** When should engagements be recorded? When met, what entry should be made? When may the entries relating to an agreement be made in the Cash Book only, and when should they be made in one's personal account?

to open a personal account with him in the Ledger. It is sufficient to debit Cash with the amount received of him. But in case the contract is more complex, and requires several entries to be made at different times, as is exemplified in my agreement with Jacob Merchant, made Nov. 10th, it becomes necessary to open a personal account with him in the Ledger, where all transactions relating to the contract should be faithfully entered.

74. Agreements should generally be made in writing, and especially when much time is to elapse before their fulfillment, or when they are in any degree complex. When this is not practicable it is desirable to make agreements in the presence of witnesses, as in case of the engagement to furnish wood, entered into Dec. 1st. In such cases the memorandum should be made as soon after the agreement as practicable, while all the particulars are fresh in the memory.

75. The Memorandum Book should be frequently reviewed to see what contracts, if any, remain to be fulfilled, when the proper entries should be made opposite such as have been performed. In cases like that entered under date Dec. 4th, the reserved space may be filled at the time the entry is made. It will generally be advisable, and especially in case your circumstances are much changed, to make out a general inventory of your property at the commencement of each year.

76. In case of a limited business, the Memorandum Book, like the Cash Book and Bill Book, may be kept in the Ledger; but it will generally be preferable to keep it in a separate book, after the manner of the one hereto annexed.

QUEST. **74.** When should agreements be made in writing? When not in writing, how may they be made? — **75.** Why should the Memorandum Book be frequently reviewed? How often should a general inventory be made? — **76.** How should the Memorandum Book be kept?

GENERAL INVENTORY OF MY PROPERTY.

January 1st, 1860.

77. Value of Farm, including

Buildings and Fixtures . .		4400.00
Value of Timber Lot . .		850.00
do. Teams and Agricultural Implements		475.00
Stock of Cattle		875.00
do. Sheep		500.00
Cash on hand		80.75
Note against Peter York . .		84.00
do. do. Ira Butts . . .		15.75
Wm. Williams owes me on Acct.		84.00
Oren Olds do. do.		15.00
Total Value of Property . .		$7379.50
I Owe as Follows:		
On Timber Lot . .	150.00	
J. Olds on Note . .	14.75	
H. Brown on Acct. .	12.50	
O. Hyde do. .	2.25	179.50
Net Capital this Day . .		$7200.00

The increase of my property since Jan. 1st, 1859, has been $450.81.

My business is in a more prosperous state than ever before, for which I have great reason to be thankful.

4th.

Engaged to furnish J. Bronson with 10 lbs. of Butter a week for family use till May 1st, for 15 cents a pound, to be paid for in cash as delivered.

May 1st, engagement fulfilled and new one entered into this day.

6th.

Commenced trading with H. Van Allen, who is to take my Wheat at cash price when delivered; likewise the crop now on the ground. For particulars see written agreement of this date.

Contract fulfilled and account settled, Dec. 29th, 1860.

January 12th, 1860. John Bruce commenced work on farm this day, for 8 months, on conditions fully set forth in our written contract. For the first three months I am to give him $10 per month, and for the remaining 5 months $11 per month. I am to give him what store pay he wants, from time to time, never exceeding his earnings, and to give him my note on settlement for any balance that may remain due, payable by the middle of November next.	Settled Sept. 12th, and gave my note to balance for $29.25, at sixty days. Paid note Nov. 12th. Bruce wishes to work for me next season. (See Arts. 36 & 65.)
Mar. 16th. Engaged to furnish Dr. J. Goodman with 95 pounds of Maple Sugar, to be paid for on delivery at 12 cents per pound.	All delivered and paid for, April 20th.
April 15th. Agreed with James Underhill to plant sixteen-acre lot (No. 7) to corn, on conditions fully set forth in contract this day made.	All obligations satisfactorily met Nov. 10th, 1860.
May 1st. Contracted to supply J. Bronson with Butter for family use till Oct. 1st, at 12 cents per pound. I have also agreed to let him have all the Cheese from my dairy, as the same shall become merchantable, to be paid for on delivery, at $6 per 100 lbs.	Contract fulfilled Nov. 1st, 1860.
14th. Engaged to put sixteen tons of hay, well cured and in good condition, into Stephen Wakeland's barn by the 15th of July, to be paid for 1st Sept. at $7.25 per ton.	Engagement met and pay received Sept. 1st, 1860.

June 7th, 1860.	
Employed Harriet Benson to do housework for 13 weeks, at $1.25 per week.	Wages paid and she left, Oct. 9th.
Sept. 15th.	
Harriet Ann has this day entered upon her duties as First Assistant in the Union School, at $15 per month, or $45 per quarter of twelve weeks.	Succeeded well. Wages paid Jan 1, 1861.
"	
Henry and Frances have this day commenced attending the Union School for the winter term.	They left school March 1st, 1861.
Nov. 10th.	
Purchased groceries for the winter of Jacob Merchant, to whom I have contracted 800 bushels of corn at 40 cents per bushel, the balance due me to be paid in cash when the full amount is delivered.	All engagements discharged. Nov. 20th, 1860.
Dec. 1st.	
Engaged to furnish Ira Wilson with 20 cords of Hickory, at $1.50 a cord, to be delivered at his house by the 15th of January, and to be paid for by the 10th of April. Present, Hiram Wilson and Jacob Townsend.	Obligations met. April 12th, 1861.
4th.	
Mill-dam carried away by a freshet, and mill much injured.	Loss $140.00.

EXAMPLES FOR PRACTICE.

FIRST FORM OF ACCOUNTS.

78. Examples for Practice are introduced into this work to enable the pupil to *reduce to practice* the knowledge of Book-keeping which he has already acquired. Each example in the First Form of Accounts consists of several transactions with the same individual, which, taken together, constitute a separate account, that should be opened, conducted, and closed, as in the case of examples already given.

79. For the purpose of solving these examples, the pupil should procure the necessary quantity of paper, ruled according to the instructions given at the 25th page, (Art. 28;) or he may make the perpendicular rulings himself. If the computations are correctly made, and the transactions are rightly entered, the last entry in the account will agree with the answer given after the last transaction in each example.

80. After each example has been solved, and the account has been accurately made out and properly balanced, the pupil will do well to copy his work neatly into Account Book No. 1, which has been prepared to accompany this volume, or into some other suitable book provided for that purpose.

EXAMPLE I.

81. This example consists of a series of transactions between the Book-keeper (each pupil may suppose himself or herself the person) and Asa P. Leonard, a country merchant.

NOTE. The Student will do well to carefully review the suggestions addressed to him on the 7th page before proceeding further. The young Teacher, also, may be aided by the suggestions addressed to him on the 9th page.

QUEST. **78.** Why are examples for practice introduced into this work? Of what does each example consist, and how should it be treated? — **79.** What suggestion is given for the pupil? How may you know whether the computations are correctly made, and the transactions rightly entered? — **80.** What suggestion is made in relation to the use of Account Books? — **81.** Of what does the first example given in the first form of accounts consist? What may each pupil suppose himself?

Transaction 1. Jan. 4, 1860. I have sold Asa P. Leonard one quarter of Beef, weighing 150 lbs. for five cents a pound. I have received in partial payment 2 lbs. of Black Tea at 70 cents a pound; 4 lbs. of Coffee at 14 cents a pound; and 25 lbs. of Brown Sugar at 10 cents a pound.

Tr. 2. Jan. 25. I have bought of Asa P. Leonard three gallons of Molasses at forty-four cents a gallon.

Tr. 3. Feb. 10. Sold him 40 lbs. of Pork worth eight cents a pound. Received of him forty dollars in Cash.

Tr. 4. Feb. 15. I have sold him fourteen bushels of Corn at forty-five cents a bushel.

Tr. 5. May 10. I have plowed his Garden, for which I am to receive one dollar and seventy-five cents.

Tr. 6. May 15. I have sold him eighteen bushels of Potatoes at thirty-five cents a bushel.

Tr. 7. June 12. Sold him 250 lbs. of Wool at forty cents a pound. Received of him 18 yards of Calico at 15 cents a yard, and three papers of pins at five cents each.

Tr. 8. July 12. Have done two days' Work with Team, for which I am to receive one dollar and seventy-five cents a day.

Tr. 9. Nov. 1. I have pastured his Cow fourteen weeks, for which he is to pay me 20 cents a week.

Tr. 10. Dec. 4. I have this day finished drawing him twenty-four cords of Beech and Maple, for which I am to receive one dollar and fifty cents a cord. I have bought of him one pair of Kip Brogans for $1.25; 18 lbs. of Rice at six cents a pound; 9 lbs. Loaf Sugar at 14 cents a pound; and 9 yards of Merrimack Sheeting at 9 cents a yard.

Tr. 11. Dec. 29. I have this day settled with him and received the balance due me in Cash. What will be my last credit entry? *Ans.* $114.32.

NOTE. The solution of this example is given on the 6th and 7th pages of the Key. To find the solution of any other example, look, as in this case, immediately under the title of the account, in the Key, for the page or pages upon which the example is recorded in the Book-keeping, which are there given in the same type with this Note.

6 61

EXAMPLE II.

82. This example consists of a series of transactions with O. D. Knowlton, a saddle and harness maker.

Transaction 1. Jan. 4, 1860. Sold O. D. Knowlton eight bushels of Potatoes at thirty-five cents a bushel, and four bushels of Corn at forty-two cents a bushel.

Tr. 2. Feb. 10. Sold him ten bushels of Potatoes for thirty-five cents a bushel, and twelve bushels of Wheat at eighty-seven and a half cents a bushel.

Tr. 3. May 1. Sold him sixteen pounds of Butter at twelve and a half cents a pound. Bought of him one set of Double Harness, valued at thirty dollars.

Tr. 4. May 6. Sold him fourteen bushels of Corn, for which he is to pay me forty-five cents a bushel.

Tr. 5. June 10. Sold him four bushels of Potatoes at thirty-five cents a bushel. Also, bought of him one Brass Plated Single Harness, at thirty-five dollars.

Tr. 6. July 2. Bought of him one Saddle, Bridle, and Martingale, the whole for eighteen dollars and fifty cents.

Tr. 7. July 10. I have sold him ten tons of Hay at four dollars and twenty-five cents a ton.

Tr. 8. Sept. 25. I have pastured four Cows for him ten weeks, for which I am to receive twenty cents a week for each Cow; also, one Horse nine weeks, at twenty-five cents a week. We this day settle, and I pay him the balance due him in Cash. How much do I pay him? *Ans.* $2.57.

EXAMPLE III.

83. This example consists of a series of transactions with Isaac Mitchell, who keeps a boot and shoe store.

Transaction 1. Jan. 1, 1860. I have bought of Isaac

QUEST. **82.** Of what does the second example consist? — **83.** Of what does the third example consist?

Mitchell one pair of Kip Boots for three dollars, and one pair of Buffalo Over Shoes at two dollars and fifty cents.

Tr. 2. Jan. 10. I have sold him two and a half dozen Hens' Eggs at fourteen cents a dozen.

Tr. 3. Feb. 10. Have sold him four pounds of Butter at 15 cents a pound, and two bushels of Wheat at 75 cents a bushel. Have bought of him one pair of India Rubber Over Shoes for $1.25, and one pair of Buckskin Mittens for 75 cents.

Tr. 4. March 4. Have sold him one quarter of Beef, weighing 175 lbs., for 5 cents a pound. Have bought of him one pair of Congress Gaiters for $3.00; two pairs of Misses' Gaiters at $1.25 each; and two pairs of Children's Gloves at 15 cents a pair.

Tr. 5. May 14. Have sold him 18 lbs. of Wool for 30 cents a pound, and 14 lbs. of Butter at 11 cents a pound. Bought of him two pair of R. R. Jenny Linds at $1.25 a pair; one pair of Enameled Gaiters at $2.50; and six Linen Handkerchiefs at 60 cents each.

Tr. 6. June 5. Have bought of him two pairs of Boys' Suspenders, at 15 cents a pair, and three pairs of Mixed Half Hose at twenty cents a pair.

Tr. 7. June 10. Have bought of him one Leghorn Hat for $1.50; two pairs of Calf Buskins for $1.00 a pair; and three pairs of Black Cotton Hose at 25 cents a pair. I have this day settled my account with Mitchell and paid him the amount due. What was it? *Ans.* $8.91.

EXAMPLE IV.

84. This example exhibits a Sheep and Wool Account. In this account the cost of the sheep, and every thing paid out on their account, should be entered on the Dr. side. On the Cr. side of the account should be entered every thing that

QUEST. **84.** What does the fourth example exhibit?

is received on account of the sheep, including the value of wool on hand, surviving sheep, and lambs.

Transaction 1. June 1, 1859. I have bought one hundred and sixty Sheep at one dollar and twenty-five cents a head, for which I have paid the cash.

Tr. 2. Dec. 15. The Sheep have been in pasture since their purchase for six and one half months. Pasturing is estimated at three dollars a month for one hundred Sheep, and at the same rate for any greater number.

Tr. 3. March 15, 1860. The Sheep have been fed on hay for three months. Feed and care are estimated at $12.00 a month for one hundred Sheep, and are computed at the same rate for a greater number.

Tr. 4. June 1. The Sheep have been in pasture since March 15th, at the rates specified in the second transaction. Washing and shearing have cost me at the rate of $6.00 for 100 Sheep.* I have cut from the flock six hundred pounds of Wool worth forty cents a pound. There are one hundred and fifty-two old Sheep living, worth one dollar and twenty-five cents a head, and sixty-four Lambs, worth seventy-five cents each. What must be entered on the Dr. side in closing the account, as the profit on one hundred and sixty Sheep for one year? *Ans.* $153.60.

EXAMPLE V.

85. The fifth and sixth examples consist of a series of transactions with Henry Webster, a bookseller and stationer. The account, which was settled July 10th, was reopened the 10th of September. If the sixth example is entered on the same folio with the fifth, the name of Henry Webster

* This account should, under this date, be debited with the interest on the cost of one hundred and sixty sheep for one year, which is computed at seven per cent.

QUEST. **84.** What should be entered on the Dr side of this account? What on the Cr. side? — **85.** Of what do the fifth and sixth examples consist?

need not be written the second time, but the account may be reopened, after the manner of the continuation of the account with John Martin, as given at the 42d and 43d pages.

Transaction 1. Jan. 1, 1860. I have sold Henry Webster 15½ lbs. of Butter for 14 cents a pound, and 25 lbs. of Cheese at 8 cents a pound. I have bought of him one Family Bible at $3.00; one Webster's Dictionary at $3.50; and one copy of Mayhew on Education for $1.00.

Tr. 2. Jan. 5. Sold Henry Webster forty pounds of Butter at fourteen cents a pound.

Tr. 3. Jan. 10. Bought of him one Thomson's Higher Arithmetic for 75 cents; one Smith's Arithmetic for 50 cents; and two Tower's Intellectual Algebra, at 37½ cents each.

Tr. 4. June 4. Sold him ten pounds of Linen Rags at four cents a pound. Bought of him four quires of Writing Paper at 20 cents a quire; two Tower's Gradual Reader at 25 cents each; and two copies of Webster's Spelling Book at ten cents each.

Tr. 5. July 1. Sold him 10 pounds of Butter at 10 cents a pound, and 4 doz. Hens' Eggs at 8 cents a dozen. Bought of him one Wells' Grammar at 38 cents, and two copies of Thomson's Practical Arithmetic at 38 cents each.

Tr. 6. July 10. Settled and paid the amount due him in cash. How much was it? *Ans.* $0.65.

EXAMPLE VI.

86. This example consists of a series of transactions with Henry Webster, the bookseller and stationer named in the last preceding example. (See Art. 85.)

Transaction 1. Sept. 10, 1860. Sold Henry Webster 25 bushels of Potatoes at 30 cents a bushel, and ten pounds of Butter at 12½ cents a pound. Bought of him two quires

---

Quest. 86. If the account with an individual is settled and balanced, and subsequently reopened on the same folio, is it necessary to write his name the second time?

of Writing Paper at 25 cents each; one Ackerman's Natural History for 50 cents; and one Day Book and one Ledger, each containing five quires of paper, at 34 cents a quire.

Tr. 2. Nov. 1. Bought of him one Thomson's Higher Arithmetic, one Davies' University Arithmetic, and one Perkins' Higher Arithmetic, at seventy-five cents each.

Tr. 3. Nov. 10. Bought of him one Smith's Astronomy for seventy-five cents, and two copies of Guernsey's History of the United States at sixty-two and a half cents each.

Tr. 4. Dec. 12. Finished drawing twenty cords of Beech and Maple at two dollars and twenty-five cents a cord.

Tr. 5. Dec. 15. Bought 4 quires of Writing Paper at 20 cents, and one Sons of Temperance Offering for $2.25.

Tr. 6. Dec. 20. Bought one North American Second Class Reader for 50 cents; one Ivory Folder for 19 cents; and one Box of Wafers for six cents. Settled, and received the balance due me in Cash. How much was it?

Ans. $41.30.

EXAMPLE VII.

87. The seventh example exhibits a Pork Account, and the eighth a Beef Account. The entries are to be made according to the principles stated under the fourth example, and more fully elucidated under the account with a Wheatfield, given at the 34th and 35th pages. (See Arts. 39 and 84.)

Transaction 1. Sept. 10, 1860. I have bought forty-five Hogs weighing 9856 lbs. at three cents a pound.

Tr. 2. Sept. 15. I have bought 17 Hogs weighing 4180 lbs. at $2\frac{3}{4}$ cents a pound. I have bought for their feed 900 bushels of Corn at forty cents a bushel.

Tr. 3. Oct. 25. Paid six cents a bushel for moving and grinding 280 bushels of Corn, to be used for feed.

QUEST. 87. What do the seventh and eighth examples exhibit? In these and similar accounts, how are we to determine what transactions to enter on the Dr. and what on the Cr. side of the account?

Tr. 4. Dec. 10. The expense of slaughtering sixty-two Hogs may be estimated at seventy-five cents each.

Tr. 5. Dec. 11. I have laid by for family use 750 lbs. of Pork which is worth five cents a pound.

Tr. 6. Dec. 12. The expense of marketing 62 Hogs is estimated at 20 cents each. I have sold 18,650 lbs. of Pork for five cents a pound. What has been the profit on fattening sixty-two Hogs? *Ans.* $123.67.

EXAMPLE VIII.

88. This example exhibits the particulars of a Beef Account. (For instructions see Arts. 39 and 84.)

Transaction 1. July 20, 1859. Bought twenty-one Yoke of Oxen at sixty-eight dollars a yoke.

Tr. 2. Aug. 4. Bought 15 Cows at twelve dollars a head.

Tr. 3. Aug. 10. Bought 22 Cows at $12.50 a head.

Tr. 4. Aug. 20. Bought 23 Steers at $20.00 a head.

Tr. 5. Nov. 1. The pasturing up to this time is estimated at eleven weeks for all of the cattle, (some have been kept longer and others not so long,) and at twelve cents a week per head. They have up to this time been fed one hundred loads of pumpkins worth 50 cents a load.

Tr. 6. Feb. 1, 1860. Have fed one hundred tons of hay worth four dollars and fifty cents a ton; also 1800 bushels of corn worth thirty-five cents, and have paid for grinding the same five cents a bushel. Have this day sold the whole, at the following prices: Twenty-one yoke of Oxen, each Ox weighing 980 lbs., at five cents a pound; thirty-seven Cows at an average weight of 600 lbs. for four and one half cents a pound; and twenty-three Steers weighing 700 lbs. each, at five cents a pound. What has been the profit on fattening Beef? *Ans.* $164.36.

NOTE. For the advantages attendant upon keeping this class of accounts see Arts. 39 and 40. See also the Note on the 71st page.

EXAMPLE IX.

89. This example consists of a series of transactions with F. M. Granger, a saddle and harness maker.

Transaction 1. Jan. 4, 1860. Bought of him one common one-half tug Harness for $16.00; three common Halters at 75 cents each; and two common Bridles at 75 cents each.

Tr. 2. Jan. 10. Sold him ten cords of Wood for $2.25 a cord, and 18 bushels of Potatoes at 30 cents a bushel.

Tr. 3. Jan. 25. Sold him 20 lbs. of table Butter for which he is to pay me fourteen cents a pound.

Tr. 4. Feb. 10. Sold him eighteen bushels of Wheat at one dollar and thirty-eight cents a bushel.

Tr. 5. Feb. 26. Have this day delivered to him 25 lbs. table Butter at fifteen cents a pound.

Tr. 6. March 4. Sold him 2 tons of Hay at $4.50 a ton.

Tr. 7. March 22. Have this day delivered to him 10 bushels of Potatoes at thirty-five cents a bushel.

Tr. 8. April 10. Bought of him one common Saddle at $7.00; one quilted Saddle at $25.00; and one pair of Martingales at seventy-five cents.

Tr. 9. June 6. Bought of him one Buggy Harness, black trimmings, at $20.00; one common Single Harness for $13.00; and two Bridle Halters at $1.20 each.

Tr. 10. June 10. Sold him 10 bushels of Wheat at one dollar and forty cents a bushel.

Tr. 11. July 2. Bought of him one Plated Buggy Harness for $25.00, and one light Double Harness with Turrets and Hooks, for $30.00. Have done for him four days' work with team, worth $2.00 a day.

Tr. 12. July 24. Have pastured two Cows for him 12 weeks, at 20 cents per week for each Cow.

Tr. 13. Nov. 15. Have had Collars repaired for thirty-eight cents, and bought a Throat-latch for twenty cents.

Tr. 14. Nov. 25. Have furnished him 10 bushels of Wheat at $1.38 a bushel; 80 lbs. of Butter at 14 cents a pound; and 75 lbs. of Cheese at 7 cents a pound. Bought of him one Hard Leather Trunk for twenty dollars.

Tr. 15. Dec. 1. Sold him 4 tons of Hay at $5.00 a ton.

Tr. 16. Dec. 20. He has trimmed my Buggy for which I am to pay him $18.00, and repaired a Buggy Harness for $2.25. I have bought of him one Long Tug Harness for $24.00, and one Bridle Halter for $1.20.

Tr. 17. Dec. 30. Have this day settled with him and paid him $10.09 in Cash, and given him my Note to balance, at thirty days. What was the face of the Note?

Ans. $50.00.

EXAMPLE X.

90. This example relates to a Field of Oats of Five Acres. The account is kept in all respects like that with a Wheatfield, given at the 34th and 35th pages. (Art. 39.)

Transaction 1. April 20, 1860. Have spent 5 days with team in plowing for oats. Labor is worth $2.00 a day.

Tr. 2. April 26. Have furnished 18 bushels of Oats for Seed, worth 31 cents a bushel; and have devoted three-fourths of the day to sowing the same, labor being worth $1.00 a day.

Tr. 3. April 27. A boy and team have been occupied two days in harrowing in oats, at $1.50 a day.

Tr. 4. July 20. Have devoted five days to harvesting field of oats, which is worth $1.25 a day.

Tr. 5. Sept. 22. Have this day finished threshing 200 bushels of oats, the entire amount raised from the field. Threshing costs six cents a bushel.

Tr. 6. Oct. 26. Have devoted three days to marketing 200 bushels of oats, which, including the use of team, is worth three cents a bushel. The crop has been raised on land worth $20.00 an acre, and has required the use of it one

QUEST. **90.** To what does the tenth example relate? How is the account kept?

year, money being worth 7 per cent. per annum. Received for the oats this day sold, 25 cents a bushel; retained straw for fodder, worth $5.00; and received $3.00 for straw sold to the upholsterer. What profit on this Field of Oats?

Ans. $7.42.

EXAMPLE XI.

91. This example exhibits an account with a Wheatfield of Sixty Acres. The value of land and the rate of interest are the same as stated in the last example.

Transaction 1. June 25, 1859. Have finished plowing the field of sixty acres, which was worth $1.75 an acre.

Tr. 2. July 20. Have finished harrowing the field, which was worth thirty-three and one-third cents an acre.

Tr. 3. Sept. 10. Have finished the cross-plowing, which was worth one dollar and twenty-five cents an acre.

Tr. 4. Sept. 15. Have furnished 90 bushels of seed wheat, which was worth 75 cents a bushel. Sowed the field, which was worth 10 cents an acre; and harrowed after the sowing, which was worth 75 cents an acre.

Tr. 5. July 10, 1860. Have this day finished cradling, binding, and shocking the sixty acres of wheat, which was worth one dollar an acre.

Tr. 6. July 14. Have finished drawing into the barn, which was worth thirty-three and one-third cents per acre.

Tr. 7. Aug. 1. Have paid 10 cents a bushel for threshing. The field yielded fifteen hundred bushels of wheat.

Tr. 8. Aug. 15. Marketed 1350 bushels, the time and trouble being worth 2 cents a bushel. The value of the land per acre, and the rate of interest as already stated. Kept for use on the farm, one hundred bushels of seed wheat, worth 75 cents a bushel; reserved for family use 50 bushels, worth 75 cents a bushel; and sold, at the same price, 1350

QUEST. 91. What account is exhibited in the eleventh example? What was the value of the land occupied, and what the rate of interest charged for its use?

bushels. Sold $20.00 worth of straw to the paper-maker, and kept $10.00 worth for fodder. What has been the profit on this field of wheat? *Ans.* $495.50.

EXAMPLE XII.

92. This example exhibits an account with a Potato Field of Twenty Acres, the land being worth thirty dollars an acre; interest at 7 per cent. (See Art. 39.)

Transaction 1. May 1, 1860. The plowing of the twenty acres for potatoes was worth one dollar and fifty cents an acre.

Tr. 2. May 10. Have furnished 225 bushels of potatoes for seed, which were worth 30 cents a bushel. The planting cost one dollar and fifty cents an acre.

Tr. 3. June 25. I have spent ten days with boy and horse in plowing out potatoes, which was worth $1.25 a day. I have also paid for thirty days' work in hoeing, at seventy-five cents a day.

Tr. 4. Nov. 1. The digging required 70 days' labor, worth 75 cents a day; the marketing required 10 days with team, at $2.00 a day; and the value of the land and the rate of interest as already stated. Sold 2450 bushels of potatoes for 25 cents a bushel; used 200 bushels in fattening hogs, worth 15 cents a bushel; and reserved 600 bushels for home use, worth 25 cents a bushel. What has been the net profit on this Potato Field for one year? *Ans.* $515.50.

NOTE. During the nine years the former editions of this work have been before the public, the author has received many communications from practical Farmers, and from the officers of Agricultural Societies, assuring him of the numerous and great advantages they believe to have resulted from the introduction of the foregoing Examples for Practice; and as he has also been many times assured of the lively interest with which pupils generally engage in their solution, he has retained them almost unchanged in the present *revised edition*. Similar features have likewise been incorporated into subsequent forms of account.

QUEST. **92.** What does the twelfth example exhibit? What was the value of the land, and what the rate of interest? What net profit on this crop?

SECOND FORM OF ACCOUNTS.

93. In every form of keeping accounts the *principle* is the same. The Second Form of Accounts differs from the First in but few particulars. In the *second form* there are *two sets of money columns on each page*, while in the *first form* there is but *one set* on a page. In the second form, also, the debits and credits are both kept on the same page, and entered in the order of their occurrence, the debits in the left-hand set of money columns, and the credits in the right-hand set.

94. On the next page is the account with Henry Van Allen, given from the 42d to the 45th pages, (which see,) here arranged according to the provisions of the Second Form of Accounts. This method requires less space for an account than where two pages are employed, and especially where there is a considerable inequality in the number of entries on the two sides of the account; but there is a greater liability to make mistakes in entering the amounts in the correct set of money columns.

95. The First Form of Accounts is adapted to the wants of farmers generally, and of persons who have but a limited amount of business to transact. The Second Form is often used by mechanics and physicians, and by merchants doing a small business. But the Third Form is better adapted to the wants of persons extensively engaged in any of the foregoing employments. And Double Entry will often be found preferable to either, and especially in a complicated business.

QUEST. **93.** Is the *principle* the same in every form of accounts? In what particulars does the *second form of accounts* differ from the *first?* — **94.** What account already given is here arranged according to the provisions of the Second Form of Accounts? What are the advantages, and what the disadvantages, of this method? — **95.** To whose wants are the different Forms of Account adapted, and by whom are they used?

Henry Van Allen Dr. Cr.

1860.			$	cts.	$	cts.
Jan.	6	To 2¼ Yds. Broadcloth 4.00	9	00		
"	"	" 2½ " Cassimere 2.30	5	75		
"	"	" Trimmings for Clothes	4	25		
"	10	By 20 Bushels Wheat .75			15	00
Feb.	4	To 40 lbs. Brown Sugar .08	3	20		
"	"	" 30½ Yds. Sheeting .10	3	05		
"	"	" 10 " DeLaine .34	3	40		
"	"	" Trimmings . . .		31		
Apr.	9	" 4 Yds. Irish Linen .56	2	24		
"	"	" 1½ " Linen Edging .20	.	30		
May	10	" 2 Linen Hdkfs. .37½		75		
"	"	" 16 Yds. Wat'd Silk 1.25	20	00		
"	"	" 1 Pair Kid Buskins	1	25		
July	1	" 30 Yds. Sheeting .11	3	30		
"	"	" 14 lbs. Loaf Sugar .14	1	96		
Aug.	4	" 2 Palm Leaf Hats .31¼		63		
"	10	" 10 Yds. Brown Linen .35	3	50		
"	"	" 24 " L. Gingham .31	7	44		
Oct.	12	" 4 " Broadcloth 3.00	12	00		
"	"	" 1⅙ Doz. Buttons .25		29		
"	"	" Trimmings per Bill	12	25		
"	15	By 90 Bushels Wheat .87			78	30
Dec.	29	" Cash to Balance .			1	57
			94	87	94	87

By referring to the remarks made upon this account at the 44th and following pages, the learner will be prepared to answer the subjoined questions. (Arts. 50 and 51.)

Quest. **95.** What should the books of the Creditor specify? What of the last Dr. entry in the account with H. Van Allen? May the Debtor give credit in his books per bill received? In such cases what should be done with the bill? Why should the items sold be specified in the books of the Creditor, when they may be entered per bill in the books of the Debtor? What rule is given for making Dr. and Cr. entries?

97. This example is the same as that given at the 48th page, but differently arranged. As here presented, it is receipted by James Armitage, the merchant, per Bulkley, his clerk, June 2d, 1860. As before presented it was not receipted.

98. In this form of an Account Current, the transactions, like the entries in the Second Form of Accounts, are recorded *in the order of their occurrence*, the amounts in all cases being carried to the Dr. or Cr. columns, as circumstances require.

99. In consequence of the greater liability to make mistakes in carrying the amounts to the correct set of money columns, as already intimated, the learner should be doubly careful that his entries are correctly made, until the *habit of accuracy* is firmly established; and then he should not relax his efforts. With the practical book-keeper, *accuracy* is of the first importance; for the detection of a few mistakes in an account, or even of but one mistake, tends greatly to diminish the confidence that might otherwise be reposed in him. The learner, hence, can not labor too assiduously in establishing a habit that will be of so great importance to him in all future life, whether engaged in business for himself or for others.

100. On the next page are two examples, which will sufficiently illustrate this mode of making out accounts. They are the same as those given at the 49th page, with the transactions arranged to compare with the Second Form of Accounts. Here, as before, the price and the quantity are given, and the pupil is left to carry out the amount. He should be careful to carry each amount to the right set of money columns. If the amounts are correctly entered, the accounts will exactly balance. (See instructions, pp. 7 and 9.)

QUEST. **97.** As here presented, how is it receipted?—**98.** In this form of accounts, how are the transactions recorded? To what columns are the amounts carried? In which set of money columns should the debits be entered, the right or the left? In which set should the credits be entered?—**99.** Why should the learner be doubly careful in making these entries? How long should he thus be careful? Should he then relax his efforts? What is said of the importance of *accuracy*?—**100.** When price and quantity are given, what should the pupil do?

James Farmer,
In Acct with Ira Merchant, Dr. Cr.

1860.			Dr. $	cts.	Cr. $	cts.
Jan.	10	To 3½ Yds. Flannel .50	---	---		
"	"	" 6 " Calico .15	---	---		
"	"	" 7¾ " Shirting .16	---	---		
"	"	By 9 Bushels Oats .23				---
May	4	To 1 Hoe, per son John		88		
"	"	By 4 Doz. Hens' Eggs .09				---
June	10	To 2 Scythes and Snaths	3	50		
"	16	By 8 Doz. Hens' Eggs .08				---
July	1	" Cash to Balance			5	20
			---	---	---	---

(Example 1.)

Isaac Paywell,
In Acct. with Ira Merchant, Dr. Cr.

1860.			Dr. $	cts.	Cr. $	cts.
Feb.	12	By 40 Bushels Oats .27			---	---
"	"	" 12 do. Corn .44			---	---
"	15	" 60 do. Wheat .84			---	---
Mar.	10	To 4 Yds. Broadcloth 4.50	---	---		
"	"	" 16 " Black Silk 1.00	---	---		
"	"	" Cash to Balance	32	48		
			---	---	---	---

(Example 2.)

QUEST. **100.** What will be the footings in the first example when the amounts are carried out and added? What in the second example?

EXAMPLES FOR PRACTICE.

SECOND FORM OF ACCOUNTS.

101. As the remarks made under this head at the 60th page are applicable to the examples that follow, the pupil will do well to review them before proceeding further. The former examples were solved according to the First Form given for keeping accounts; these are to be solved according to the Second Form of Accounts. (See Arts. 78 and 79.)

EXAMPLE I.

102. This example consists of a series of transactions with James Davidson, who keeps a grocery and provision store. (For instructions see Note at Art. 81.)

Transaction 1. Jan. 2, 1860. Bought of him 18 lbs. Brown Sugar at 8 cents a pound; 15 lbs. of Rice at 7 cents a pound; and 12 lbs. of Loaf Sugar at 14 cents a pound.

Tr. 2. Feb. 10. Paid him four dollars in Cash. Also, bought of him 10 lbs. of Codfish at six cents a pound, and 2 gallons of Molasses at forty-four cents a gallon.

Tr. 3. March 4. Bought of him 12 lbs. of Butter at 15 cents a pound, and 10 lbs. of Cheese at 8 cents a pound.

Tr. 4. March 24. Bought of him 8 lbs. of Corn Starch at 11 cents a pound; 2 lbs. of Saleratus at 9 cents a pound; and 4 lbs. of Ginger at 10 cents a pound.

Tr. 5. April 12. Bought of him 4 bushels of Potatoes at 42 cents a bushel, and 6 doz. Eggs at 10 cents a dozen. Paid him on account four dollars in Cash.

Tr. 6. May 1. Have this day purchased of him one Ham, weighing 18 lbs., at 9 cents a pound, and 14 lbs. of Corn Meal at one cent a pound.

QUEST. **101.** Why are examples for practice introduced into this work? Of what does each example consist, and how should it be treated? How may you know whether the computations are correctly made, and the transactions rightly entered? —**102.** Of what does the first example in the second form of accounts consist?

Tr. 7. June 10. Bought this day of James Davidson 12 lbs. of Rice at 6 cents a pound.

Tr. 8. July 2. Bought one-half bushel of Potatoes at 50 cents a bushel, and 10 lbs. of Mackerel at 9 cents a pound.

Tr. 9. Aug. 1. Settled and paid the balance due him in Cash. How much was it? *Ans.* $7.62.

EXAMPLE II.

103. This example consists of five transactions with Henry Ingalls, who keeps a boot and shoe and furnishing store.

Transaction 1. Jan. 4, 1860. I have sold him 8 cords of Hickory at $1.50 a cord. Have bought of him 1 pair of Kip Boots for $4.00; 3 pairs of Children's Gaiters at 60 cts. a pair; and 2 pairs of Boys' Suspenders at 14 cts. a pair.

Tr. 2. April 10. Purchased of him this day three pairs of Children's Gloves at fifteen cents a pair.

Tr. 3. April 14. Bought of him 4 Linen Hdkfs. at 60 cents each, and 2 pairs of Misses' Gaiters at $1.25 a pair.

Tr. 4. May 6. Bought one Leghorn Hat for one dollar and fifty cents, and 2 Palm Leaf Hats for 30 cents each.

Tr. 5. May 20. Sold him 80 lbs. of Wool for 40 cents a pound, and settled the account, he paying the balance due in Cash. What was the amount paid by him to balance the account? *Ans.* $30.47.

EXAMPLE III.

104. This example consists of a series of transactions with John Adams, a hardware merchant.

Transaction 1. Jan. 10, 1860. Bought of him 2 Axes at $1.25 each, and 3 Ax Helves at 20 cents each.

Tr. 2. April 4. Bought of him three shanked Hoes at 65 cents each, and one Hoe with welded eye for 44 cents.

Tr. 3. June 10. Bought 3 Scythes at eighty-eight cents each, and 2 Scythe Snaths at seventy-five cents each.

QUEST. **103.** Of what does the second example consist? — **104.** Of what the third.

Tr. 4. June 20. Bought a Log Chain weighing 20 lbs., at 10 cents a pound, and one Bush Scythe for one dollar.

Tr. 5. July 2. Bought of him one Grain Cradle for three dollars, and two Hay Rakes for fifteen cents each.

Tr. 6. Sept. 10. Settled and paid the amount due him in Cash. How much was it? *Ans.* $15.93.

EXAMPLE IV.

105. This example consists of a Tobacco Account for the period of twelve years. The person whose account is here presented uses three Cigars a day, that cost him three cents apiece, and pays for Tobacco in other forms, for Smoking and Chewing, $4.59 a year. This is a low estimate of the expenses of an habitual smoker and chewer of Tobacco. Thousands of persons that support these habits pay on their account twice or thrice the amount here stated. Compute the pecuniary expense incurred at this estimate, on account of these habits, in twelve years, allowing interest on the amount invested at 7 per cent. with annual settlements.

The transactions, which we will suppose commenced with the beginning of the year 1841, may be arranged as follows:

Transaction 1. 1841. At the end of the year there should be entered on the Dr. side of the account the amount expended for Cigars and Tobacco for one year.

Tr. 2. 1842. At the end of this year there should be entered on the same side of the account, first the interest* on the amount expended for the *preceding* year, and then the amount expended for the last year.

Tr. 3. 1843. At the end of this year there should be entered, first the interest on the amount expended for the

* In computing interest, if the mills and decimals amount to *more than half a cent*, count them as a cent; if they amount to *less than half a cent*, omit them entirely.

QUEST. **105.** Of what does the fourth example consist? What number of Cigars are used a day, and at what cost, and what amount of Tobacco does the person whose account is here presented use? Is this a high estimate?

two preceding years, (the interest on the sum expended the first year being considered a part of said amount,) and then the amount expended for the last year.

Tr. 4. 1844. There should be entered, first the interest on the amount expended for the *three* preceding years, (the interests that have accrued being considered a part of said amount,) and then the amount expended for the last year.

Tr. 5. 1845. There should be entered, first the interest on the amount expended for *all the preceding years,* (the interests that have accrued being considered a part of said amount,) and then the amount expended for the last year.

[The preceding transactions sufficiently elucidate the principle upon which the remaining seven transactions should be entered, the last of which will be as follows:]

Tr. 12. 1852. There should be entered, first the interest on the amount expended for the *eleven* preceding years, (the interests that have accrued being considered a part of said amount,) and then the amount expended for the last year. Finally, the account should be closed by entering on the Cr. side the necessary amount to balance. (Art. 33.) What will be the expense of these two habits in twelve years, as deduced from these transactions? *Ans.* $669.75.

EXAMPLE V.

106. The Tobacco Account introduced in the last example is here continued. That account was for the period of twelve years. This example brings the account down eleven years further, making twenty-three years in all. Like the former, it will require twelve transactions, of which the first two and the last are here given.

Transaction 1. 1852. There should be entered on the Dr. side of the account the amount expended for Tobacco the first twelve years, as shown by the preceding example.

QUEST. **105.** What is the expense incurred by an individual for Tobacco on account of Smoking and Chewing according to this estimate in twelve years?

[The first entry is neither more nor less than the "amount to balance" the preceding account brought forward.]

Tr. 2. 1853. There should be entered, first the interest on the amount expended for Tobacco the *twelve* preceding years, and then the amount expended for the last year.

Tr. 12. 1863. This transaction should be entered on the principle stated in the twelfth transaction of the last example.

[The principle upon which the intervening transactions should be entered has been sufficiently elucidated.]

What will be the expense of Smoking and Chewing, at the rates stated in Example IV., for the period of twenty-three years? *Ans.* $2000.65.

EXAMPLE VI.

107. The Tobacco Account embraced in the two preceding examples is here continued. In those two examples taken together, the account is exhibited for twenty-three years; in this it is brought down eleven years further, making thirty-four years in all. It will require the same number of transactions as the last example. These will commence with the year 1863, and end with the year 1874.

What will be the expense of Smoking and Chewing, at the rates stated in Example IV., for the period of thirty-four years? *Ans.* $4802.01.

EXAMPLE VII.

108. This example consists of the Cash Account of an individual who is employed at a salary of $500.00 a year. In the 11th and 19th transactions the articles purchased are not specified; but there is reference to a Memorandum Book in which they are supposed to be entered.

Transaction 1. Jan. 1, 1860. The individual debits Cash

QUEST. **106.** What will the expense amount to in twenty-three years, according to this estimate? — **107.** What in thirty-four years? — **108.** Of what does the seventh example consist?

with the amount of Cash on hand at the beginning of the year, which is twenty-five dollars and fifty cents.

Tr. 2. Jan. 29. Paid 4 weeks' board at 2 dollars a week.

Tr. 3. Feb. 27. Paid 4 weeks' board at 2 dollars a week.

Tr. 4. Mar. 25. Paid 4 weeks' board at 2 dollars a week.

Tr. 5. April 1. Received one quarter's salary.

Tr. 6. April 10. Paid 30 dollars for a suit of clothes.

Tr. 7. April 24. Paid four weeks' board at 2 dollars a week. Also paid the same day 4 dollars for one silk hat.

Tr. 8. May 3. Paid a missionary subscription of $15.00.

Tr. 9. May 10. Have this day subscribed and paid ten dollars for the support of the ministry the current year.

Tr. 10. May 23. Paid 4 weeks' board at $2.00 a week.

Tr. 11. June 1. Paid for sundries for personal use, as per memorandum, four dollars and fifty-six cents.

Tr. 12. July 4. Paid anniversary expenses, amounting in all to four dollars and fifty-seven cents.

Tr. 13. July 22. Paid 8 weeks' board at $2.00 a week.

Tr. 14. Aug. 15. Received 1 and a half quarter's salary.

Tr. 15. Aug. 25. Bought a dress and sundry small articles for sister, amounting in all to $12.50.

Tr. 16. Oct. 1. Received one half quarter's salary.

Tr. 17. Oct. 10. Paid $14.00 for a cow for my mother.

Tr. 18. Oct. 22. Paid 13 weeks' board at $2.00 a week.

Tr. 19. Nov. 10. Bought sundries as per memorandum, amounting to seven dollars and seventy-five cents.

Tr. 20. Dec. 31. Paid 11 weeks' board at $2.00 a week. Received one quarter's salary. What amount of Cash on hand? *Ans.* $319.12.

EXAMPLE VIII.

109. This example exhibits a Wine Account for the period of twelve years. It embraces the amount paid for Wine, Cigars, etc., and occasionally a moderate expenditure

QUEST. **109.** What does the eighth example exhibit? What does it embrace?

for a social repast, including supper, cards, and sundry kindred disbursements. The expense is estimated at $1.00 a day, which a reformed man (who has had twenty years' experience, during which time he squandered an immense patrimony) informs me is a very low estimate of the expenses attendant upon fashionable tippling. Interest is to be computed as in the Tobacco Account exhibited in Example IV., and the transactions are to be entered according to the principles there stated.

110. The Wine Account, we will suppose, commenced with the year 1848. What will it amount to in twelve years ending with the year 1859? *Ans.* $6529.29.

EXAMPLE IX.

111. The Wine Account introduced in the last example is here continued. That account was for the period of twelve years. This example brings the account down eleven years further, making twenty-three years in all. This, like Example V., will embrace twelve transactions. These commence with the year 1859, and include the year 1870.

What will the Wine Account amount to in twenty-three years? *Ans.* $19,504.22.

EXAMPLE X.

112. The Wine Account embraced in the two preceding examples is here continued. In those two examples taken together, the account is exhibited for twenty-three years; in this it is carried forward eleven years further, making thirty-four years in all. It will require the same number of transactions as the last example. These will commence with the year 1870 and end with the year 1881. What will the Wine Account amount to in thirty-four years? *Ans.* $46,814.55.

QUEST. **109.** What is the expense estimated at per day? Is this a high estimate? —**110.** What will the account amount to in twelve years? —**111.** What in twenty-three years? —**112.** What will the Wine Account amount to at this rate in thirty-four years?

EXAMPLE XI.

113. This example and the next consist of a series of transactions with Otho H. Hudson, a hardware merchant.

Transaction 1. Jan. 3, 1860. Bought of him 2 Nail Hammers at 50 cents each; one Cast Steel Nail Hammer at one dollar; 2 Hand Saws at $2.00 each; one large Backed Saw for $2.00; and one small Backed Saw for $1.25.

Tr. 2. Feb. 1. Bought of him 2 Jack Planes and 2 Fore Planes at $1.25 each, and 2 Long Jointers at $1.50 each.

Tr. 3. Feb. 10.. Bought 1 pair of Match Planes, 1¼ in., for $2.00; 2 pairs of Match Planes, 1½ in., at $2.25 a pair; and 2 Smoothing Planes at $1.00 each. Paid $8.00 on acct.

Tr. 4. March 20. Bought of him one seven-foot Cross-cut Saw at 63 cents a foot, and one seven-foot Mill Saw at 94 cents a foot. Settled and paid him the balance due in Cash. How much was it? *Ans.* $28.74.

EXAMPLE XII.

114. This example is a continuation of the account with Otho H. Hudson, introduced in the last example.

Transaction 1. April 1, 1860. Bought of him 2 Bed-cords at 25 cents each; one Dinner-bell at one dollar; one Clothes-brush at 50 cents; one Nail-brush at 31 cents; and 2 Tooth-brushes at 20 cents each.

Tr. 2. May 10. Bought of him one Strainer Milk-pail for 60 cents; 3 Milk-pans at 20 cents each; and one Wire Sieve for 44 cents. Settled and paid the amount due on the account. How much was it? *Ans.* $4.35.

EXAMPLE XIII.

115. This example consists of a Sheep and Wool Account. I give it as furnished by a citizen who kept the Sheep. The transactions may be arranged under two dates.

QUEST. **113.** What do the eleventh and twelfth examples consist of? — **115.** Of what does the thirteenth example consist?

Transaction 1. June, 1859. I have thirty Sheep, chiefly Lambs, valued at one dollar and twenty-five cents each.

Tr. 2. June, 1860. The Sheep have been kept a portion of the year on a summer-fallow, where they were rather useful to the fallow than expensive, and the remainder of the year on the common. The pasturing and care may be considered worth $4.80 for the year. They were not foddered at all; but during the winter they were fed half a bushel of oats a day for 60 days, oats being worth 25 cents a bushel. The expense of washing and shearing was 4 cents a head. The marketing of the Wool was worth 50 cents. Had the sheep been sold a year ago, the money would have drawn 10 per cent. interest. Kept 7 lbs. of Wool, worth 40 cents a pound, for family use. Sold 103 lbs. for 40 cents a pound. The 30 old Sheep are worth $1.50 each. I have raised 27 Lambs from them, worth $1.25 each. What has been the profit on 30 Sheep for one year? *Ans.* $67.50.

EXAMPLE XIV.

116. This example is an acct. with O. D. Morgan, a grocer.

Transaction 1. Jan. 25, 1860. Bought of him 10½ lbs. of Brown Sugar at 10 cents a pound; 12 lbs. of Butter at 14 cents; and 4 bushels of Potatoes at 40 cents a bushel.

Tr. 2. Feb. 20. Bought of him 8 lbs. of Rice at 6 cents a pound, and 12 lbs. of Corn Starch at 12½ cents a pound.

Tr. 3. May 2. Bought of him 8 lbs. of Codfish at 6 cents a pound. Settled and paid the amount due in Cash. How much money did he receive? *Ans.* $6.79.

NOTE. The 13th example, on page 84, is similar to the examples referred to in the note at the 71st page. Such examples may with equal propriety be kept by the First Form of Accounts, or by the Second Form.

QUEST. **115.** Is it real or fictitious? What was the profit on thirty Sheep for one year? How much is this a head?

Transaction 1. June, 1859. I have thirty Sheep, chiefly Lambs, valued at one dollar and twenty-five cents each.

Tr. 2. June, 1860. The Sheep have been kept a portion of the year on a summer-fallow, where they were rather useful to the fallow than expensive, and the remainder of the year on the common. The pasturing and care may be considered worth $4.80 for the year. They were not foddered at all; but during the winter they were fed half a bushel of oats a day for 60 days, oats being worth 25 cents a bushel. The expense of washing and shearing was 4 cents a head. The marketing of the Wool was worth 50 cents. Had the sheep been sold a year ago, the money would have drawn 10 per cent. interest. Kept 7 lbs. of Wool, worth 40 cents a pound, for family use. Sold 103 lbs. for 40 cents a pound. The 30 old Sheep are worth $1.50 each. I have raised 27 Lambs from them, worth $1.25 each. What has been the profit on 30 Sheep for one year? *Ans.* $67.50.

EXAMPLE XIV.

116. This example is an acct. with O. D. Morgan, a grocer.

Transaction 1. Jan. 25, 1860. Bought of him $10\frac{1}{2}$ lbs. of Brown Sugar at 10 cents a pound; 12 lbs. of Butter at 14 cents; and 4 bushels of Potatoes at 40 cents a bushel.

Tr. 2. Feb. 20. Bought of him 8 lbs. of Rice at 6 cents a pound, and 12 lbs. of Corn Starch at $12\frac{1}{2}$ cents a pound.

Tr. 3. May 2. Bought of him 8 lbs. of Codfish at 6 cents a pound. Settled and paid the amount due in Cash. How much money did he receive? *Ans.* $6.79.

NOTE. The 13th example, on page 84, is similar to the examples referred to in the note at the 71st page. Such examples may with equal propriety be kept by the First Form of Accounts, or by the Second Form.

QUEST. **115.** Is it real or fictitious? What was the profit on thirty Sheep for one year? How much is this a head?

that the work has been reviewed. When thus tested, the *amount* of the purchase or sale may be *full extended.* In this form of accounts it is customary to use the counting-room *at* (@) in connection with the price per yard, pound, etc.

122. The LEDGER is a book to which the entries recorded in the Day Book are transferred, and so arranged as to present the account with each person on a folio by itself.

123. The Ledger is ruled as follows: Each page is divided by double perpendicular lines into two equal parts, each of which is ruled like the Ledger in the First Form of Accounts, with this exception: there is an additional space at the left of the money columns in which is entered the page of the Day Book from which the entry is posted.

124. The *amount only* of the articles purchased at any one time is carried to the Ledger. The debit entry, "To Day Book, 21, $5.38," which is the first in the following Ledger in the account with H. M. Roberts, is elliptical, (see p. 100.) Supply the ellipses and the entry stands thus: "To the amount of the articles debited in the Day Book on the 21st page, $5.38." The same is true of all Ledger entries.

125. Instructions are sometimes given to note in connection with debit and credit entries in the Ledger, the words "Sundries," "Groceries," "Goods," "Merchandise," "Cash," "Note," "Order," etc., as the case may be. This may properly be done whenever such an entry will save the necessity for referring to the Day Book for an explanation; for we should keep as few books as will answer our purpose, and with the least writing practicable make them tell the most possible. But as such entries give the Ledger a bad appearance, they should be employed only when useful.

QUEST. **121.** What is said of the counting-room *at* (@) used in the third form of accounts? — **122.** What is the Ledger? — **123.** How is it ruled? What is the use of the additional space? — **124.** In posting, what only is carried to the Ledger? What is said of elliptical entries? How will it stand with the ellipses supplied? Is the same true of all Ledger entries? — **125.** What instructions are sometimes given in relation to posting? When may this be done, and why?

126. Moreover, to avoid the common inconvenience in text-books of turning the book around in order to exhibit the Ledger accounts, which is both unnatural and awkward, and the scarcely less objectionable method of exhibiting the Dr. and Cr. entries on different pages, which is rarely if ever practiced in this form of accounts, it has been found necessary to diminish the third space in the Ledger, and to use the letters *D. B.* instead of the whole word Day Book. We likewise employ *B.* for Balance, *I.* for Invoice, *I. B.* for Invoice Book, *S. B.* for Sales Book, and *P. & L.* for Profit & Loss, and for a like reason. But in doing this, while we really sacrifice nothing, we gain much; for we exhibit the exact form in which accounts are usually kept. Indeed, many of our best accountants omit this space entirely. It will be seen, then, that the middle course has been adopted in this treatise.

127. Posting Books is transferring the accounts of various persons from the Day Book, through which they are scattered, to the Ledger, and arranging each on a folio by itself, with the proper reference figures in the Day Book to show the folio of the Ledger *into* which each entry is posted, and with corresponding reference figures in the Ledger to show the page of the Day Book *from* which each entry is posted.

128. Posting is done as follows: Take the Day Book and turn to the first unposted entry, and by means of the Index find the account in the Ledger to which the entry belongs, if such an account has been opened. If no such account has been opened in the Ledger, write the proper title in the Index, opposite which place the folio of the Ledger that is to be devoted to the account, and then, having entered the title in the Ledger, proceed with the posting. Entries may be posted directly from the Cash Book.

Quest. **126.** What do the letters *D. B.* in the third space in the Ledger stand for? What do other letters named stand for? Why has this abridgment been made? What is sacrificed, and what gained by it? — **127.** What is meant by the term *Posting Books?* — **128.** How is Posting done?

129. If at any time it is ascertained that a transaction has not been recorded in its proper place, and under its appropriate date, the entry should be immediately made, with the proper explanation. In the First and Second Forms of Account, the first entry of an account will of course be made in the Ledger, as that is the only book used; but in the Third Form of Accounts the original entry should in all cases be made in the Day Book, from which it must be posted into the Ledger.

130. Should an entry at any time, by accident or carelessness, be made on the wrong side of an account, it should not be erased; but the same amount should be entered on the opposite side of the account, "To Error," or "By Error," as the case may be. It is apparent that the only effect of this last entry will be to *counteract the mistake;* this done, the correct entry should be made. In case a transaction is entered to the wrong account, the correction is made in a similar manner; but too great pains can not be taken to make the original entries correct. It should be the aim and pride of the book-keeper *never to make a mistake in the entry of his accounts.*

131. It has been already remarked, (Art. 29,) that when a person has several Ledgers, they should be designated by the letters of the alphabet, thus: Ledger A; Ledger B; etc. Day Books should be lettered in the same manner; and the first entry that is posted from a *new* Day Book into the Ledger should show in the Ledger the Day Book from which it

QUEST. **129.** If at any time it is ascertained that a transaction has not been recorded in its proper place, and under its appropriate date, what should be done? Where is the first entry of an account made in the First and Second Forms of Account? Where in the Third Form of Accounts? — **130.** In case a transaction is entered on the wrong side of an account, should the entry be erased? What should be done? What will be the effect of this entry? Should the correct entry then be made? In case a transaction is entered to the wrong account, how is the correction made? Can too great pains be taken to make the original entries correct? What should be the aim and pride of the book-keeper? — **131.** When several Day Books and Ledgers are used by the same person, how are they designated? When you commence to post from a *new* Day Book, what should the first entry show?

is posted. For example, if you commence Day Book A, and Ledger A, at the same time, the Day Book may be filled when the Ledger is not more than one-fourth full. In this case the first entry to each account that is posted from Day Book B into Ledger A should be entered thus: *To* or *By* (as the case may be) *Day Book* B, *p.* 1.

132. When one Ledger is filled and a new one is opened, any unsettled accounts may be carried to the new Ledger in the same manner that an account is carried from one folio to another, for which see Arts. 48 and 49.

ILLUSTRATIVE EXAMPLE.

THIRD FORM OF ACCOUNTS.

133. For the purpose of illustrating the mode of making Day Book entries and posting the same into the Ledger, we introduce a *sample* of Transactions as taken from a Retail Store, with the Day Book entries and Ledger postings which these Transactions require. The learner has only to suppose himself the *merchant* conducting this business, and to regard these Transactions as having *actually occurred*, and they will possess for him nearly all the advantages of *real business.* He will thus have the benefit of combining the Theory of business with Practice in the counting-room, as fully as is possible short of engaging in actual business.

Tuesday, May 1st, 1860.

Transaction 1. I have sold to H. M. Roberts 28 yds. of Sheeting at eight and a half cents a yard, and two pairs of Shoes at one dollar and fifty cents a pair; and I have received from him 22 bushels of Oats at 45 cents a bushel.

QUEST. **131.** Give an example.—**132.** When one Ledger is filled and a new one opened, what should be done with unsettled accounts?—**133.** For what purpose are sample transactions introduced? What should the learner do, and with what advantage to himself?

Tr. 2. I have received from Isaac Hinman 20 lbs. of Butter at 15 cents a pound, and two Hams, together weighing 44 lbs., at 12½ cents a pound; and I have sold him 3 shanked Hoes at 60 cents each.

Wednesday, May 2d, 1860.

Tr. 3. Have sold to Bronson Fisher 20 Seamless Bags at 22 cents each; one grain Scoop Shovel at one dollar; and 14 lbs. of Rope at 15 cents a pound.

Thursday, May 3d, 1860.

Tr. 4. Have sold to James Ellis one Pocket Compass for 50 cents; 2 pairs of Snuffers at 37½ cents each; and a Pocket Knife worth one dollar.

Tr. 5. N. O. Morehouse has bought of me 2 Brooms at 15 cents each; 7 yards of Gingham at 22 cents a yard; 10¾ yards of Blue Drill at 16 cents a yard; and 2 Scythe Stones at 10 cents a piece.

Friday, May 4th, 1860.

Tr. 6. A. F. Kingsley has bought of me 2 pairs of Spring Dividers at 63 cents a pair; 2 Trunk Locks at 31 cents each; and one Chest Lock worth 44 cents.

Saturday, May 5th, 1860.

Tr. 7. I have sold to Silas Boomer 2 Dead Locks at 62½ cents each; 2 Cottage Locks at $1.50 each; and 3 Trunk Locks worth 35 cents apiece.

Monday, May 7th, 1860.

Tr. 8. Bronson Fisher has purchased of me 2 Sprinkling Pots at 38 cents each; one Buck Saw worth $1.00; and one Box of 8 x 10 Glass worth $2.25.

Tr. 9. James Sterling has bought of me two Handsaw Files at 10 cents each; one set of Knives and Forks for $1.15; and 12 lbs. of Lead Pipe at 8 cents a pound. I have received of him one quarter of Beef weighing 210 lbs. at 5 cents a pound.

Tuesday, May 8th, 1860.

Tr. 10. I have sold to H. M. Roberts 15 lbs. of Brown Sugar at 10 cents a pound, and $7\frac{3}{4}$ yards of Calico at 16 cents a yard. I have bought of him 14 bushels of Potatoes at 40 cents a bushel.

Thursday, May 10th, 1860.

Tr. 11. I have sold Isaac Hinman 12 yards of Shirting at $12\frac{1}{2}$ c. a yard, and $6\frac{3}{4}$ yds. of Sheeting at 9 c. a yd.

134. From these transactions and the entries based upon them in the annexed Day Book, the learner will at once see what must have been the transactions requiring the remaining Day Book entries. As an exercise, private learners and classes may profitably examine these Day Book entries, and state or write out in common language the transactions upon which they are based.

135. This Illustrative Example commences with the 21st page of the Day Book, and continues to the 26th page, which we will call Day Book A. These Day Book entries are posted to pages 34, 35, and 36 of the Ledger, which, as we have already had three Ledgers, we will call Ledger D.

136. Day Book entries are made at the time and in the order of occurrence of the transactions upon which they are based. The figures in the column at the left of these entries are inserted *at the time of posting*, and they indicate the pages of the Ledger to which the entries are posted. In like manner the figures at the left of the money columns in the Ledger indicate the pages of the Day Book from which the several entries to an account have been posted.

QUEST. **134.** What do the transactions stated, and the entries based upon them, show? What exercise is suggested? — **135.** Where does the *illustrative example* introduced commence, and what space does it occupy? — **136.** When are Day Book entries made? When are the figures at the left of these entries inserted, and what do they indicate? What do corresponding figures in the Ledger indicate?

Albion, Tuesday, May 1st, 1860.

	H. M. Roberts — Dr.				
34	To 28 Yds. Sheeting @ 8½ c.	2	38		
	" 2 Pairs Shoes @ 1.50 .	3	00	5	38
	Cr.				
34	By 22 Bushels Oats @ 45 c. .			9	90
	"				
	Isaac Hinman — Cr.				
34	By 20 lbs. Butter @ 15 c. .	3	00		
	" 2 Hams, 44 lbs. @ 12½ c.	5	50	8	50
	Dr.				
34	To 3 Shanked Hoes @ 60 c.			1	80
	Wednesday, May 2d.				
	Bronson Fisher — Dr.				
	To 20 Seamless Bags @ 22 c.	4	40		
34	" 1 Grain Scoop Shovel	1	00		
	" 14 lbs. Rope @ 15 c. .	2	10	7	50
	Thursday, May 3d.				
	James Ellis — Dr.				
	To 1 Pocket Compass . .		50		
35	" 2 Pr. Snuffers @ 37½ c.		75		
	" 1 Pocket Knife . .	1	00	2	25
	"				
	N. O. Morehouse — Dr.				
	To 2 Brooms @ 15 c. . .		30		
35	" 7 Yds. Gingham @ 22 c.	1	54		
	" 10¾ Yds. Blue Drill @ 16 c.	1	72		
	" 2 Scythe Stones @ 10 c.		20	3	76

Albion, Friday, May 4th, 1860.

	A. F. Kingsley Dr.		
	To 2 Pr. Spring Dividers @ 63	1 26	
36	" 2 Trunk Locks @ 31 c.	62	
	" 1 Chest Lock . . .	44	2 32
	— Saturday, May 5th. —		
	Silas Boomer Dr.		
	To 2 Dead Locks @ 62½ c.	1 25	
36	" 2 Cottage do. @ 1.50	3 00	
	" 3 Trunk do. @ 35 c.	1 05	5 30
	— Monday, May 7th. —		
	Bronson Fisher Dr.		
	To 2 Sprinkling Pots @ 38 c.	76	
34	" 1 Buck Saw . . .	1 00	
	" 1 Box 8×10 Glass . .	2 25	4 01
	— " —		
	James Sterling Dr.		
	To 2 Handsaw Files @ 10 c.	20	
35	" 1 Set Knives and Forks	1 15	
	" 12 lbs. Lead Pipe @ 8 c.	96	2 31
	— Cr. —		
35	By 1 Qr. Beef, 210 lbs. @ 5 c.		10 50
	— Tuesday, May 8th. —		
	H. M. Roberts Dr.		
34	To 15 lbs. Brown Sugar @ 10 c.	1 50	
	" 7¾ Yds. Calico @ 16 c.	1 24	2 74
	— Cr. —		
34	By 14 Bush. Potatoes @ 40 c.		5 60

	Isaac Hinman Dr.				
34	To 12 Yds. Shirting @ 12½ c.	1	50		
	" 6¾ Yds. Sheeting @ 9 c.		61	2	11
	—— // ——				
	James Ellis Dr.				
35	To 1 Framing Chisel ½ in.		50		
	" 2 do. do. ¾ in. @ 75c.	1	50		
	" 1 Cow Bell		75	2	75
	—— Cr. ——				
35	By Repairs on Store, per Bill			4	50
	—— Saturday, May 12th. ——				
	N. O. Morehouse Cr.				
35	By 6 Bushels Wheat @ 1.75			10	50
	—— Dr. ——				
	To 10½ lbs. Cast Steel @ 22 c.	2	31		
35	" 14 " German do. @ 15 c.	2	10	4	41
	—— Monday, May 14th. ——				
	A. F. Kingsley Dr.				
36	To 1 Set Knives & Forks	1	25		
	" 1 Quart Measure . .		26	1	51
	—— Cr. ——				
36	By 2 Cords Beech Wood @ 1.75			3	50
	—— // ——				
	Silas Boomer Dr.				
36	To 2 Stand Lamps @ 37½c.		75		
	" 2 Wheel Heads @ 25 c.		50		
	" 1 Pocket Compass . .		40	1	65

24 Albion, Thursday, May 17th, 1860.

L.F.	Entry	$	c.	$	c.
	James Sterling Dr.				
35	To 12 lbs. Raisins @ 12½ c.	1	50		
	" 3½ Galls. Molasses @ 56 c.	1	96	3	46
	Cr.				
35	By 1 Quarter Veal, 18 lbs. @ 5 c.				90
	Saturday, May 19th.				
	H. M. Roberts Dr.				
	To 2 Sets Coffee Cups @ 1.00	2	00		
34	" 1 Split Broom . . .		25		
	" 3 Common do. @ 20 c. .		60	2	85
	Monday, May 21st.				
	Isaac Hinman Dr.				
34	To 1 Set Knives and Forks	1	50		
	" 15 lbs. Coffee @ 18 c. .	2	70	4	20
	Thursday, May 24th.				
	James Ellis Dr.				
	To 2 Pocket Knives @ 37½ c.		75		
35	" 2 Vest Patterns @ 2.25	4	50	5	25
	Delivered to Son Robert				
	Saturday, May 26th.				
	N. O. Morehouse Dr.				
	To 1 Spice Mill . . .		75		
35	" 2 Sets Knitting Pins @ 9 c.		18		
	" 3 Wheel Heads @ 50 c.	1	50	2	43
	Cr.				
35	By 20 lbs. Butter @ 16 c. .	3	20		
	" 4 Bushels Wheat @ 1.75	7	00	10	20

Fol.	Entry	$	¢	$	¢
	H. M. Roberts Dr.				
34	To 14 lbs. Java Coffee @ 20 c.	2	80		
	" Cash to Balance . .	1	73	4	53
	—— Monday, June 4th. ——				
	Isaac Hinman Cr.				
34	By 75 lbs. Wool @ 42 c. .			31	50
	—— Dr. ——				
	To my Note @ 30 Days .	30	00		
34	" Cash to Balance . . .	1	89	31	89
	—— " ——				
	Bronson Fisher Cr.				
34	By 60 lbs. Wool @ 45 c. .			27	00
	—— Dr. ——				
	To 3 Pitchforks @ 50 c. . .	1	50		
34	" 1 Grain Cradle . . .	2	25		
	" 4 Hay Rakes @ 25 c. .	1	00		
	" Cash to Balance . .	10	74	15	49
	—— Wednesday, June 6th. ——				
	James Ellis Cr.				
35	By 2 Days' Work @ 1.50	3	00		
	" 200 ft. Pine Bds. @ 20. per M.	4	00	7	00
	—— " ——				
	N. O. Morehouse Cr.				
35	By 40 lbs. Wool @ 40½ c.			16	20
	—— Dr. ——				
35	To paid his Order to J. Brown	6	30		
	" Cash to Balance . .	20	00	26	30

Albion, Friday, June 8th, 1860.

	James Sterling Dr.				
	To 1 Umbrella	1	63		
35	" 2 Parasols @ 1.75 . .	3	50	5	13
	Delivered to Daughter Jane				
	—— Monday, June 11th. ——				
	A. F. Kingsley Dr.				
36	To his Order to H. Allen			12	00
	—— " ——				
	Silas Boomer Dr.				
	To 2 Scythes @ 1.13 . .	2	26		
36	" 4 do. Stones @ 10 c.		40		
	" 2 do. Snaths @ 50 c.	1	00	3	66
	—— Thursday, June 14th. ——				
	James Sterling Dr.				
	To 24 lbs. Crushed Sugar @ 10 c.	2	40		
35	" 2 Gallons Molasses @ 56c.	1	12	3	52
	—— Monday, June 18th. ——				
	A. F. Kingsley Dr.				
35	To 14 lbs. Java Coffee @ 15 c.	2	10		
	" 10 lbs. Rice @ 7 c. . .		70	2	80
	—— Cr. ——				
36	By Note to Balance . .			15	13
	—— Wednesday, June 20th. ——				
	Silas Boomer Dr.				
	To 4 lbs. Ginger @ 15 c. .		60		
36	" 6 lbs. Corn Starch @ 12 c.		72		
	" 8½ lbs. Candles @ 14 c.	1	19	2	51

INDEX TO LEDGER D.

Letters	Name	Page	Letters	Name	Page
A B	*Boomer, Silas*	36	M	*Morehouse, N. O.*	35
C D E	*Ellis, James*	35	N O		
F	*Fisher, Bronson*	34	P Q		
G H	*Hinman, Isaac*	34	R	*Roberts, H. M.*	34
I J			S	*Sterling, James*	35
K	*Kinsley, A. F.*	36	T U V		
L			W X Y Z		

34 **Dr. H. M. Roberts Cr.**

1860.						1860.					
May	1	To D.*	21	5	38	May	1	By D.	21	9	90
"	8	"	22	2	74	"	8	"	22	5	60
"	19	"	24	2	85						
June	1	"	25	4	53						
				15	50					15	50

Dr. Isaac Hinman Cr.

1860.						1860.					
May	1	To D.	21	1	80	May	1	By D.	21	8	50
"	10	"	23	2	11	June	4	"	25	31	50
"	21	"	24	4	20						
June	4	"	25	31	89						
				40	00					40	00

Dr. Bronson Fisher Cr.

1860.						1860.					
May	2	To D.	21	7	50	June	4	By D.	25	27	00
"	7	"	22	4	01						
June	4	"	25	15	49						
				27	00					27	00

* D. B., or D. only, as here employed, stands for Day Book.

Dr. James Ellis Cr.

1860.						1860.					
May	3	To D.	21	2	25	May	10	By D.	23	4	50
"	10	"	23	2	75	June	6	"	25	7	00
"	24	"	24	5	25						
June	30	Balance		1	25						
				11	50					11	50
						June	30	Balance		1	25

Dr. N. O. Morehouse Cr.

1860.						1860.					
May	3	To D.	21	3	76	May	12	By D.	23	10	50
"	12	"	23	4	41	"	26	"	24	10	20
"	26	"	24	2	43	June	6	"	25	16	20
June	6	"	25	26	30						
				36	90					36	90

Dr. James Sterling Cr.

1860.						1860.					
May	7	To D.	22	2	31	May	7	By D.	22	10	50
"	17	"	24	3	46	"	17	"	24		90
June	8	"	26	5	13	June	30	Balance		3	02
"	14	"	26	3	52						
				14	42					14	42
June	30	Balance		3	02						

36 **Dr. A. F. Kingsley Cr.**

1860.						1860.					
May	4	To D.	22	2	32	May	14	By D.	23	3	50
"	14	"	23	1	51	June	18	"	26	15	13
June	11	"	26	12	00						
"	18	"	26	2	80						
				18	63					18	63

Dr. Silas Boomer Cr.

1860.											
May	5	To D.	22	5	30						
"	14	"	23	1	65						
June	11	"	26	3	66						
"	20	"	26	2	51						
		13.12									

NOTE. The learner should not pass from the examination of this Illustrative Example till he is entirely familiar with the mode of entering these transactions in the Day Book, posting them into the Ledger, and closing the several accounts. When he is able readily to answer the following questions, and clearly to explain the processes required, he may rest assured that his subsequent progress, if equally thorough, will be easy and satisfactory.

QUEST. **136.** What is the date of the last entry posted to the account of H. M. Roberts? What are the *items* of this entry? How is the amount of "Cash to Balance" ascertained? ☞ Let the learner answer the same questions in relation to the accounts of Isaac Hinman, Bronson Fisher, and N. O. Morehouse. What is the date of the last entry posted to the account of A. F. Kingsley? What are the *items* of this entry? What is the date of the last entry posted to the account of James Ellis? This account seems to be balanced, and the balance brought down, June 30th. What is the Balance, and to whom is it due? ☞ State the same particulars in relation to the account with James Sterling. What is the condition of the account of Silas Boomer?

PROOF OF POSTINGS AND BALANCES.

Day Book Drs. and Crs., June 30th, 1860.

Dr. Sums.			Cr. Sums.		
Dr. sum on page 21	20	69	Cr. sum on page 21	18	40
" " 22	16	68	" " 22	16	10
" " 23	12	43	" " 23	18	50
" " 24	18	19	" " 24	11	10
" " 25	78	21	" " 25	81	70
" " 26	29	62	" " 26	15	13
			Balance . . .	14	89
	175	82		175	82

Dr.	Ledger Balances, June 30th, 1860.			Cr.	
Jas. Sterling, p. 35	3	02	James Ellis, p. 35	1	25
Silas Boomer, p. 36	13	12	Balance . . .	14	89
	16	14		16	14

137. Above are entered the Dr. and Cr. sums on each page of the preceding Day Book, from which it appears the Drs. exceed the Crs. $14.89, as shown by the *Balance.* Now, as every Dr. sum in the Day Book has been posted to the Dr. side of the Ledger, and as every Cr. sum in the Day Book has been posted to the Cr. side of the Ledger, and as, in obtaining the Ledger Balances, equal sums have in every instance been omitted from each side of an account, the difference in the sums of the Dr. and Cr. Ledger Balances should exactly equal the Day Book Balance. As this is so, we conclude the *Postings* and *Balances* of the Ledger are correct.

QUEST. **137.** How can you know that your *postings* and Ledger *balances* are correct?

RETROSPECT AND PROSPECT.

We have thus far considered the three most common forms of keeping accounts by Single Entry Book-keeping.

The First Form presented extends from the 24th page to the 59th, in the discussion of which all the leading features of the science are explained and elucidated. Then follow Examples for Practice, extending from the 60th to the 71st page, in the course of which the principles taught are applied to the ordinary business transactions of life.

The Second Form of keeping accounts is briefly presented on the 72d and four following pages, (the principles of the science previously taught being alike applicable to this form,) and Examples for Practice similar to the preceding are then introduced, extending from the 77th to the 85th page. These two forms of keeping accounts are adapted to the wants of persons generally, transacting a limited business of almost any kind; but the former is more especially adapted to agricultural, and the latter to manufacturing pursuits, as has already been fully explained. In each of these two forms of accounts, the Ledger is the only account book required for use.

A Third Form of recording business transactions, which is sometimes called the Merchant's Form, is introduced on the 86th page. The principles taught are practically applied in an Illustrative Example commencing on the 90th page, and concluding with a new and reliable methed of testing the accuracy of Postings and Balances, as is fully exemplified on the last preceding page. This form requires the use of a Day Book and Ledger, and is adapted to a retail trade. In Single Entry it only remains to present appropriate Examples for Practice in the Third Form. These completed, Commercial Calculations, the Philosophy and Morals of Business, and the Science of Double Entry, are respectively considered.

QUEST. 137. State the substance of the retrospect and prospect given.

EXAMPLES FOR PRACTICE.

THIRD FORM OF ACCOUNTS.

138. In the First and Second Forms of Account each example consists of several transactions with the same individual. (See pp. 60th and 72d.) But in the Third Form of Accounts the transactions of the day are intermingled, being entered in the Day Book at the time and in the order of their occurrence. The following examples consist of transactions with twelve persons. These transactions should be entered in the Day Book prepared to accompany this volume, after the manner of those already given in the Illustrative Example, commencing at the 90th page. This done, they should be posted into the Ledger as those were, according to the instructions given at the 88th page. (Arts. 127 and 128.) These transactions, which commence with the month of May, 1860, continue three months.

139. Each pupil may regard himself as conducting the business here recorded. The accounts with *persons* are entered according to the instructions given in Art. 37; the account with Cash according to those given in Art. 45; and the accounts with Bills Receivable and Bills Payable as directed in Art. 64. Several of the following transactions will require an entry to two accounts, as is indicated at Tr. 3. Sometimes a Dr. or a Cr. entry, or both, will be required, and at the same time an entry in the Bill Book, as in Tr. 2. The learner will need carefully to exercise his judgment in determining what entries are required.

QUEST. **138.** In the First and Second Forms of Account, of what does each example consist? In the Third Form of Accounts, how are the transactions of the day recorded? Of what do the examples for practice in this form of accounts consist? What instructions are given for entering these transactions in the Day Book and Ledger? With what month do these transactions commence, and how long do they continue? — **139.** Who conducts this business? What principle do we observe in keeping accounts with *persons?* (Art. 37.) How is the Cash account kept? (Art. 45.) How are Bills Receivable and Bills Payable and accounts kept? (Art. 64.) Does the same transaction ever require an entry to more than one account?

INVENTORY OF PROPERTY IN TRADE.

Tuesday, May 1st, 1860.

140. Store and Ware House worth	$4200.00	
Merchandise in Store, ...	3500.00	
Cash in Safe and Bank, ...	900.00	
James Sill's Note, (No. 1,) B. B. (Art. 147,)	225.00	
Henry Hart owes me on acct., . . .	75.00	
James Farley do. do. . . .	60.00	
Total amount of my assets, ...		$8960.00

I owe as follows:

Isaac Hill for Mdse. on acct., . . .	$260.00	
Note (No. 1) to H. Smith for Mdse., B. B., (Art. 147,)	700.00	
Total amount of my debts, ...		$960.00
Net Capital in Trade, ...		$8000.00

141. Accounts should be opened with Cash, with Bills Receivable and Bills Payable, and with every person who owes us, or whom we owe on account, at the time of commencing business. (Art. 140.) These accounts should then be debited and credited from time to time, as our business transactions shall require. We should seek to make our Account Books tell the *truth*, the *whole truth*, and *nothing but the truth* relating to our business.

Wednesday, May 2d, 1860.

Transaction 1. I have sold Henry Allen 80 lbs. of Brown Sugar at 8½ cents a pound; 4 bbls. of Rock Salt at $2.25 a barrel; and 20 lbs. of Java Coffee at 20½ cents a pound.

Quest. 140. What amount of assets have I on commencing business, and in what do they consist? What is my indebtedness, and in what does it consist? — **141.** What accounts should be opened at the time of commencing business? What entries should then be made to these accounts? What should our Account Books tell?

Tr. 2. I have sold and delivered Merchandise to Job Otis to the amount of $75.00, for which he has given me his Note payable at my store June 25th, 1860. (Bills Receivable No. 2, Dr., and B. B. Art. 147.)

Tr. 3. James Sill has taken up his Note of Jan. 1st, payable at my store this day. (Bills Receivable No. 1, Cr., and Cash Dr.)

Friday, May 4th, 1860.

Tr. 4. O. H. Andrews has bought of me 3 bbls. of Salt at $1.25 a barrel, and 31½ yds. of Sheeting at 8½ cents a yard. I have received of him 4 Hams, together weighing 70 lbs., at 14 cents a pound.

Tr. 5. A. B. Lincoln has brought me 44 bushels of Corn at 45 cents a bushel, and 10 bushels of Wheat at 95 cents a bushel. He has bought of me 8¾ yds. of Cottonade at 24 c.; 4 lbs. of Black Tea at 60 c.; and 4 bbls. of Salt at $1.25.

Saturday, May 5th, 1860.

Tr. 6. I have sold to S. O. Jenkins 10 yds. of Calico at 11½ c.; 12 yds. of De Laine at 22 c.; and 6 yds. of Franklin Drill at 25 c. He has furnished me with 18 lbs. of Butter at 20½ c. per pound.

Tr. 7. A. C. Morton has bought of me 56 lbs. of Crushed Sugar at 11 c. a pound, and 20½ lbs. of Codfish at 6 c. a pound.

Monday, May 7th, 1860.

Tr. 8. Nathan Powers has bought of me 2 Scythes at $1.10 each, and one Grain Cradle for $2.50.

Tr. 9. I have sold John Ransom 2 pairs of Boots at $3.50 a pair; 8 Milk Pans at 40 c. each; and 40 yds. Three Ply Carpeting at 80 c. a yard.

Tuesday, May 8th, 1860.

Tr. 10. I have accepted and paid in Merchandise John Cooper's Order on me in favor of John Smith for $40.00. (Art. 37.)

Tr. 11. I have bought of Henry Smith on acct. a Bill of Merchandise as per Invoice No. 1, amounting to $200.00.

Tr. 12. I have paid my Note No. 1 of Feb. 8, given to H. Smith for Merchandise, mentioned in the Inventory of May 1st. The Note was for $700.00. (Bills Payable Dr. and Cash Cr.)

Thursday, May 10*th*, 1860.

Tr. 13. I have paid Isaac Hill $225.00 on acct. of Mdse. bought of him, mentioned in the Inventory of May 1st, and I have bought of a Pedler sundry articles of Mdse. amounting to $25.00, which I pay for in Cash.

Saturday, May 12*th*, 1860.

Tr. 14. I have sold Job Otis Merchandise as per Sales Book,* page 4, amounting to $265.00, for which I have received his Note payable in 30 days. (Bills Rec. No. 3.)

Tr. 15. The receipts of Cash for small sales, as per Money Drawer, and not otherwise entered, have been $25.00.

Tuesday, May 15*th*, 1860

Tr. 16. I have sold to Ellen, daughter of James Farley, on her father's account, one De Laine Shawl for $5.00, and 30 yds. of Gingham at 25 c. a yard.

Tr. 17. I have bought Merchandise of Henry Smith, as per Invoice No. 2, amounting to $225.00, for which I have given him my Note, payable the 4th day of June next. (Bills Pay. No. 2.)

Tr. 18. O. H. Andrews has bought of me one Suit of Clothes for $34.00; one China Tea Set for $13.00; 32 yds. of Carpeting at 80 c.; and 6½ yds. of Stair Carpet at 60 c.

* The quantity and price of the articles sold should be entered at length in the Sales Book. They are here omitted because of the space they would occupy.

Friday, May 18th, 1860.

Tr. 19. I have procured for S. O. Jenkins one Side Saddle worth $20.00, and one Single Harness worth $24.00, which I furnish him on account.

Tr. 20. A. B. Lincoln has purchased of me 4 Cast Steel Hoes at 75 c. each; 2 Grain Cradles at $2.25; and 4 Hay Rakes at 15 c. each.

Monday, May 21st, 1860.

Tr. 21. A. C. Morton has bought of me 12½ yds. of Gingham at 30 c., and 3 pairs of Cotton Hose at 28 c. I have paid his Order on me of this date for $65.00, in Mdse.

Tr. 22. Nathan Powers has purchased of me 28 yds. of Sheeting at 9½ c. a yard; 5 yds. of Brown Linen at 31 c.; and 1¾ doz. Buttons at 8 c. per dozen.

Tr. 23. I have sold to John Ransom 7 yds. of Checked Gingham at 30 c.; 2 pairs of Cotton Hose at 50 c.; and 2 pairs of Half Hose at 31 c. The goods were delivered to his daughter Mary.

Friday, May 25th, 1860.

Tr. 24. I have bought of Henry Smith a Bill of Mdse. on acct., as per Invoice No. 3, amounting to $140.25; and I have paid him $150.00 in Cash on account.

Tr. 25. I have sold John Cooper 30½ yds. of Brown Sheeting at 10 c. a yard, and 9½ yds. of Alpaca at 80 c. a yd.

Friday, June 1st, 1860.

Tr. 26. Received of Jacob Johnson $275.40 for a Bill of Goods sold him this day, as per Sales Book, p. 6.

Tr. 27. I have sold Merchandise, as per Sales Book, p. 8, to John Wood, amounting to $350.60, for which I have received his Note, payable the 9th of June. (Bills Rec. No. 4.)

Tr. 28. Henry Hart has bought of me one Coffee Mill at 88 c.; one pair of Kip Boots for $4.00; and 20 Seamless Bags at 25 c. each.

Monday, June 4th, 1860.

Tr. 29. I have taken up my Note to H. Smith for $225.00, this day due. (Bills Payable No. 2, and Cash.)

Tr. 30. I have sold to Henry Allen 4½ gallons of Molasses at 56 c., and 26½ lbs. of Bar Soap at 8 c.

Wednesday, June 6th, 1860.

Tr. 31. O. H. Andrews has bought of me 3 yds. of Cassimere at $1.75 a yd., and 8 yds. of Russia Sheeting at 37½ c. a yd.

Tr. 32. I have bought of Henry Smith a Bill of Merchandise on acct., as per Invoice No. 4, amounting to $280.00.

Saturday, June 9th, 1860.

Tr. 33. John Wood has paid his Note of $350.60, this day due. (Bills Rec. No. 4, and Cash.)

Tr. 34. James Farley has bought of me 44½ lbs. of Sugar at 10 c. per pound; 3 lbs. of Saleratus at 8 c.; and 27 yds. of Cotton Cloth at 9 c.

Tuesday, June 12th, 1860.

Tr. 35. I have bought, on account, a Bill of Merchandise of Isaac Hill, as per Invoice No. 5, amounting to $275.66.

Tr. 36. Job Otis has paid his Note of $265.00, this day due. (B. R. No. 3, and Cash.)

Thursday, June 14th, 1860.

Tr. 37. Henry Allen has bought of me 8 lbs. of Raisins at 18¾ c., and 41½ yds. of Sheeting at 10 c.

Tr. 38. S. O. Jenkins has bought of me 8 lbs. of Java Coffee at 18¾ c., and 25 lbs. of Coffee Sugar at 10 c.

Saturday, June 16th, 1860.

Tr. 39. The receipts of Cash for small sales, as per Money Drawer, and not otherwise entered, have been $24.50.

Tr. 40. I have sold to Henry Hart one barrel of Flour for $6.50, and 40 lbs. of Sugar at 9½ c. a pound.

Tr. 41. I have bought Merchandise of Sam Brown as per Invoice No. 6, amounting to $360.00, for which I have given him my Note, payable the 20th of July.

Monday, June 18*th*, 1860.

Tr. 42. I have received $235.50 in Cash, for Merchandise sold, as per Sales Book, p. 10.

Tr. 43. I have sold a Bill of Merchandise to John Wood, as per Sales Book, p. 12, amounting to $269.50, for which he has given me his Note, payable the 2d of July.

Tr. 44. I have this day settled my Book Acct. with Isaac Hill, and given him my Note at 30 days to balance. For what amount was the Note given? *Ans.* $310.66.

Friday, June 22*d*, 1860.

Tr. 45. A. B. Lincoln has bought of me 2 bbls. of Coarse Salt at $2.30 a barrel.

Tr. 46. F. Sill presents an Order on me drawn and signed by A. C. Morton, requesting the payment to him of $25.00 in goods, which I have accepted and paid.

Monday, June 25*th*, 1860.

Tr. 47. Job Otis has paid his Note of $75.00, given the 2d of May, and this day due. (B. R. No. 2, and Cash.) *

Wednesday, June 27*th*, 1860.

Tr. 48. A. C. Morton has bought of me 6¾ yds. of Sheeting at 9 c. a yard, and 2¾ yds. of Cassimere at $2.00 a yard.

Tr. 49. Nathan Powers has bought of me 3½ yds. black Cambric at 12 c.; 2 Linen Handkerchiefs at 35 c.; and 12 lbs. of Java Coffee at 17 c. per pound.

* In several instances, as in this case, parenthetical references have been made, with a view of suggesting to the learner the entries that are required. But he should now be prepared to enter his transactions without such aid; and the sooner he does so the better.

Friday, June 29th, 1860.

Tr. 50. I have sold to John Cooper 8 lbs. of Brown Sugar at 10 c. a lb., and 12 lbs. of Candles at 14½ c. a lb.

Tr. 51. I have sold to John Ransom 3 pairs of Cotton Hose at 50 c.; 2 pairs of Kid Buskins at $1.50; and 1⅔ doz. Buttons at 6 c.

Tr. 52. I have bought of Henry Hart 4 doz. Hens' Eggs at 16 c. a dozen, and 8 Hams, together weighing 160 lbs., at 12 c. per pound.

Saturday, June 30th, 1860.

142. The preceding transactions having been entered in the Day Book and posted to the Ledger, according to instructions already given, (Arts. 118 to 136,) the student will test the accuracy of his *postings* and *balances;* (Art. 137.) In case the Day Book entries have been correctly made, and the Ledger postings and balances are free from mistakes, there will exist the following

PROOF OF POSTINGS AND BALANCES.

Day Book Drs. and Crs., June 30th, 1860.

Dr. Sums.		Cr. Sums.	
The Dr. sum resulting from adding all the Dr. entries for May and June will be	$5767.43	The Cr. sum resulting from adding all the Cr. entries for May and June will be	$5054.80
		Balance	712.63
	$5767.43		$5767.43

QUEST. **142.** What instruction is given in Article 142?

The Dr. and Cr. sums upon the different pages of the Day Book will depend upon the number of transactions entered upon a page; but the *sum total* of Day Book Drs. and Crs. and the *balance* will be as indicated at the foot of the opposite page. As that Balance agrees with the Balance of the Ledger accounts given below, we conclude the work is right.

Dr. Ledger Balances, June 30, 1860.					Cr.
Cash	1051	00	Bills Payable	670	66
Bills Receivable	269	50	A. B. Lincoln	7	10
Henry Hart	75	34	Henry Smith	470	25
James Farley	79	62	Balance	712	63
Henry Allen	30	19			
O. H. Andrews	81	38			
S. O. Jenkins	49	60			
A. C. Morton	108	09			
Nathan Powers	12	21			
John Ransom	50	52			
John Cooper	53	19			
	$1860	64		$1860	64

143. If these results are obtained the student may consider his work right; but in case they are not obtained he should review his work. The closing balances should be entered under date of June 30th, to indicate the condition of the Ledger at the end of June. These balances should be brought down under date of July 2d, (the month coming in on Sunday,) to represent the state of the Ledger accounts at the beginning of July.

QUEST. **143.** When should the work be reviewed? Under what date should the closing balances be entered, and under what date should they be brought down?

Monday, July 2d, 1860.

Tr. 53. I have taken a commission to buy Wool for Isaac Hill. He is to furnish me money to buy with, and to pay me one cent a pound for my services in buying, storing, and shipping. He furnishes me with $1200.00 now, and is to furnish me more money as I may need it.

Tr. 54. John Wood has paid his Note of $269.50, this day due. (B. R. No. 5, and Cash.)

Tuesday, July 3d, 1860.

Tr. 55. James Farley has bought of me 2 Straw Hats at 37½ c. each, and 4 lbs. of Corn Starch at 12 c. per pound. He has brought me 190 lbs. of Wool, on account, at 40 c. a pound.

Thursday, July 5th, 1860.

Tr. 56. Henry Allen has bought of me one Grain Cradle at $2.50, and 2 Scythes at 88 c. each. He has brought me on account 165 lbs. Wool at 40 c. a pound.

Tr. 57. Nathan Powers has bought of me 4 lbs. of Wool Twine at 16 c. a pound, and 18 lbs. of Brown Sugar at 9 c.

Friday, July 6th, 1860.

Tr. 58. John Ransom has bought of me 4 lbs. of Wool Twine at 16 c. per pound, and 2 pairs of Sheep Shears at $1.25 a pair. He has brought me, on account, 24 lbs. of Butter at 14 c.

Monday, July 9th, 1860.

Tr. 59. Nathan Powers has brought me 245 lbs. of Wool, on account, at 42 c. a pound. He has bought of me, on account, 2 Cedar Pails at 75 c. each; 10½ lbs. of Sugar at 10 c. a pound; and 1 doz. Blue Plates for $1.00.

Thursday, July 12th, 1860.

Tr. 60. I have bought two lots of Wool for Cash; one

lot of 540 lbs. of O. White at 43 c. a pound, and the other lot of 600 lbs. of H. Brown, at the same price per pound.

Tr. 61. I have received of Isaac Hill $1800.00 in Cash to buy Wool with. (Transaction 53.)

Tr. 62. I have received of A. B. Lincoln, on account, 250 lbs. of Wool at 44 c.; 18 lbs. of Butter at 14 c.; and 4 doz. Hens' Eggs at 15 c.

Saturday, July 14th, 1860.

Tr. 63. John Cooper has brought me 425 lbs. of Wool, on account, at 45 c. a pound, according to agreement.

Tr. 64. O. H. Andrews has brought me, on account, 980 lbs. of Wool at 45 c. a pound. He has bought of me one remnant of Edging for 25 c.; $9\frac{5}{16}$ lbs. of Codfish at 7 c. a pound; and 32 yds. of Calico at 15 c.

Monday, July 16th, 1860.

Tr. 65. I have bought of Henry Smith, on acct., a Bill of Mdse. amounting to $475.00, as per Invoice No. 7.

Tr. 66. I have bought of A. C. Morton, on account, 440 lbs. of Wool at 42 c. a pound. I have sold him 14 lbs. of Java Coffee at 15 c. a pound; 25 lbs. of Brown Sugar at 9 c. a pound; and I have paid the balance due him in Cash. How much money did he receive? *Ans.* $72.36.

Tr. 67. James Farley has brought me 460 lbs. of Wool, for which I allow him 45 c. a pound. We settle our account, and I give him my Note to balance. For what amount is my Note given? *Ans.* $202.15.

Wednesday, July 18th, 1860.

Tr. 68. I pay my Note, No. 4, of $310.66, this day due to Isaac Hill at the Exchange Bank.

Friday, July 20th, 1860.

Tr. 69. I pay my Note, No. 3, of $360.00, given to S. Brown June 16th, and this day due.

Tr. 70. Henry Hart has brought me 196 lbs. of Wool at 40 c. a pound. We settle, and I pay him the balance his due in Coffee at 16 c. a pound. How many lbs. of Coffee does he receive? *Ans.* 19⅛ lbs.

Saturday, July 21st, 1860.

Tr. 71. S. O. Jenkins has sent me 450 lbs. of Wool, with the request that I place the same to his credit at 42 c. per lb., as per agreement, which I do.

Tr. 72. I have bought three lots of Wool, as follows: No. 1, 680 lbs. at 40 c.; No. 2, 951 lbs. at 40 c.; and No. 3, 720 lbs. at 40½ c.; for all of which I have paid the Cash.

Monday, July 23d, 1860.

Tr. 73. I have bought for Isaac Hill, under my commission of July 2d, (Transaction 53,) 7281 lbs.* of Wool, for which I have paid $3080.55. I have this day sent him the Wool, with a statement of its cost, and charged him for the same, and for my services, as per agreement referred to.

Tuesday, July 24th, 1860.

Tr. 74. Henry Allen has bought of me 10 gallons of Molasses at 44 c., and 45 lbs. of Brown Sugar at 10 c. We settle, and I pay him the balance his due in Cash. How much money does he receive? *Ans.* $22.65.

Wednesday, July 25th, 1860.

Tr. 75. I have settled with O. H. Andrews, and paid him the money for the balance his due. How much do I pay him? *Ans.* $353.92.

Thursday, July 26th, 1860.

Tr. 76. I have this day received a letter from Isaac Hill, acknowledging the receipt of Wool and my statement of July 23d. He expresses his entire satisfaction with the quality of Wool, and the prices I have paid, and encloses the balance my due on account, which I pass to his credit. How much money does he send me? *Ans.* $153.36.

* See note on page 228.

Friday, July 27th, 1860.

Tr. 77. I have sold to S. O. Jenkins one Grain Scoop Shovel for $1.25, and 3 gallons of Lamp Oil at $1.75 per gallon.

Saturday, July 28th, 1860.

Tr. 78. I have sold a Bill of Merchandise to James Sill amounting to $254.60, as per Sales Book, p. 18, for which I have received his Note, No. 6, payable at the Exchange Bank the 10th of August.

Tr. 79. I have settled with John Cooper, and paid the balance due him in Cash. How much was I in his debt?

Ans. $138.06.

Monday, July 30th, 1860.

Tr. 80. S. O. Jenkins has brought an order on me from Henry Smith for $200.00 payable in Merchandise, which I accept; but as he does not want his pay to-day, I make the proper entries to the accounts of the parties to the transaction.

Tuesday, July 31st, 1860.

144. The preceding business has been conducted three months, and I now wish to have a General Settlement, (Art. 67,) and to determine my gain or loss for this time. For this purpose I take an Inventory of Merchandise in Store, (Art. 146,) which amounts to $3675.00. The value of the Store and Warehouse is the same as stated in the Inventory, May 1st. (Art. 140.) I wish to determine three things:

1st. In what my Assets and Liabilities consist;

2d. How much I am worth as appears from the Inventory and my Ledger Accounts; and,

3d. Whether I have made or lost money during the three months I have been in trade, and how much.

---

144. For what length of time has this business been conducted? What three things do you wish to determine?

145. The student should first test the correctness of his postings and balances for July, (Arts. 142 and 143.) In obtaining the Day Book Drs. and Crs. to June 30th, there was a Dr. excess of $712.63; and there was the same Dr. excess in the Ledger Balances of that date. As this Dr. excess of the Ledger Balances is carried forward and enters into the Balances of July 31st, it becomes necessary to enter the same sum at the left hand, as the Dr. Day Book Balance at the beginning of July.

PROOF OF POSTINGS AND BALANCES.

Day Book Drs. and Crs., July 31st, 1860.

Dr. Sums.			Cr. Sums.		
Balance June 30	712	63	Cr. sums for July	8644	69
Dr. sums for July	8533	57	Balance . . .	601	51
	$9246	20		$9246	20

Dr. *Ledger Balances, July 31st, 1860.* *Cr.*

Dr.			Cr.		
Cash . . .	1782	01	Bills Payable	202	15
Bills Receivable	254	60	S. O. Jenkins	332	90
John Ransom	50	30	A. B. Lincoln	120	22
			Nathan Powers	84	88
			Henry Smith .	745	25
			Balance . . .	601	51
	$2086	91		$2086	91

QUEST. **145.** What use do you make of the Day Book balance for June in obtaining the proof for July?

INVENTORY OF PROPERTY IN TRADE.

Tuesday, July 31st, 1860.

146. Store and Warehouse, worth	$4200.00	
Mdse. in Store, per Inventory, . . .	3675.00	
Cash on hand, per Ledger, ...	1782.01	
Bills Receivable, per Ledger and B. B.,	254.60	
John Ransom owes me on Account, .	50.30	
Total amount of my assets, ...		$9961.91

I owe as follows:

Bills Payable, per B. B. and Ledger,	$202.15	
S. O. Jenkins, on Account, ...	332.90	
A. B. Lincoln, do.	120.22	
Nathan Powers, do.	84.88	
Henry Smith, do.	745.25	
Total amount of my Debts, ...		$1485.40
Net Capital, July 31st, 1860, ...		$8476.51
" " May 1st, "		8000.00
Have made in Trade, ...		$476.51

The Inventory of a person's property does not strictly belong to either Day Book or Ledger. It should, however, be regularly taken and carefully entered in the Memorandum Book, where it becomes a matter of permanent record. (Arts. 71 to 77.) Inventories thus made and kept, in connection with one's account books, present a complete history of his business for a series of years, which sometimes becomes a matter of importance.

QUEST. **146.** Does the Inventory of one's property belong to his Day Book or Ledger? When should it be taken, and where should it be entered? What is said of a history of one's business?

Notes and Bills

No.	Date.		Maker's Name.	Indorser's Name.
	1860.			
1	Jan.	4	James Sill	S. Osgood
2	May	2	Job Otis	P. Brown
3	"	12	Job Otis	None
4	June	1	John Wood	H. Allen
5	"	18	John Wood	None
6	July	28	James Sill	None

Notes and Bills

No.	Date.		Payee's Name.	Indorser's Name.
	1860.			
1	Feb.	4	Henry Smith	Cook & White
2	May	15	Henry Smith	None
3	June	16	Sam Brown	Cook & White
4	"	18	Isaac Hill	None
5	July	16	James Farley	None

147. At the time these Notes were received and given all of the above entries were made, except those under the head of "Remarks." These were entered as the Bills were paid. Bill Receivable No. 6 is not due at the time of my General Settlement, July 31st. The same is true of Bill Payable

QUEST. **147.** What entries should be made in the Bill Book at the time Notes are given and received? What Notes entered in the above Bill Book are not due?

Receivable.

Where Payable.	When due.		Amount.		Remarks.
	1860.				
My Store	*May*	*2*	*$225*	*00*	*Paid May 2*
do.	*June*	*25*	*75*	*00*	*Paid June 25*
do.	*"*	*12*	*265*	*00*	*Paid June 12*
do.	*"*	*9*	*350*	*60*	*Paid June 9*
do.	*July*	*2*	*269*	*50*	*Paid July 2*
Exc. Bank	*Aug.*	*10*	*254*	*60*	

Payable.

Where Payable.	When due.		Amount.		Remarks.
	1860.				
Exc. Bank	*May*	*8*	*$700*	*00*	*Paid May 8*
do.	*June*	*4*	*225*	*00*	*Paid June 4*
My Store	*July*	*20*	*360*	*00*	*Paid July 20*
Exc. Bank	*"*	*18*	*310*	*66*	*Paid July 18*
My Store	*Aug.*	*15*	*202*	*15*	

No. 5. There is, therefore, no occasion for an entry to either under the head of "Remarks." When these Notes mature the proper entries should be made under this head, showing whether they have been paid, or renewed, or otherwise disposed of, and how.

QUEST. 147. When these notes mature what entries should be made? Does this statement agree with your Ledger account?

AUXILIARY BOOKS.

148. It has already been stated that in the Third Form of Accounts two principal books are used. These are the Day Book and the Ledger. (Art. 117.)

149. AUXILIARY BOOKS are assisting or helping books. The most important of these are, the Cash Book, the Bill Book, and the Memorandum Book, which have already been described; to which may be added the Letter Book, the Invoice Book, and the Sales Book.

150. The CASH BOOK is a book in which is kept an account of all moneys received, and of all moneys paid out. (For the manner of keeping the C. B., see Arts. 45 to 47.)

151. The BILL BOOK is a book in which is kept a memorandum of Notes, Bills Receivable, Bills Payable, and Bills of Exchange. (For a fuller description of the Bill Book, and the manner of keeping it, see Arts. 60 and 147.)

152. The MEMORANDUM BOOK is used for recording memorandums of various kinds, agreements, and all important particulars relating to a person's business that belong neither to the Day Book nor Ledger. (For a full description of the Memorandum Book, see Arts. 71 to 77.)

153. The LETTER BOOK contains copies of all business letters, which ought always to be written in a neat and legible hand, and to be as clear and concise as possible. By using a Copying Machine much labor may be saved in keeping this book, and at the same time perfect accuracy secured. Copies of letters thus taken afford better evidence before a legal tribunal, than the most perfect copies made with the pen. The Letter Book should contain copies of all important business letters.

QUEST. **148.** What are the two principal books in the Third Form of Accounts? — **149.** What are auxiliary Books? What are the most important of them? — **150.** What is the Cash Book? — **151.** What is the Bill Book? — **152.** For what is the Memorandum Book used? — **153.** What does the Letter Book contain? How ought letters to be written? What of a copying machine? What of evidence in courts?

154. Good letter-writing is a fine accomplishment. The following specimen is therefore subjoined for the purpose of exhibiting the date, (1,) address, (2,) body of the letter, (3,) subscription, (4,) inscription, (5,) and superscription, (6.)

LETTER OF INTRODUCTION.

(1) *Detroit, Michigan, July 25th, 1860.*

(2) *Gentlemen:*

(3) *Allow me to introduce to your enterprising House my young friend, Timothy Trusty, of this city, who visits Boston for the purpose of procuring a situation in a Book-Publishing Establishment. From a knowledge of his uniform kindness and obedience as a son; of his industry and attainments as a student; of his proverbial honesty and truthfulness; and of his many amiable qualities, I think him such a person as you will be pleased to employ, in case you need additional help; and I therefore take great pleasure in introducing him to your favorable acquaintance.*

(4) *I remain, Gentlemen,*

Yours, very respectfully,

Ira Mayhew.

(5) *Messrs. Chase, Nichols & Hill,*

43 Washington St., Boston, Mass.

QUEST. **154.** What is said of good letter-writing? For what purpose is a specimen of letter-writing introduced? Do the traits of character attributed to the person described in this letter of introduction entitle him to confidence and esteem? What are some of these traits of character?

155. Below is exhibited the correct form of a letter when folded. The superscription (6) should occupy the lower half of the letter or envelope, both on account of its appearance, and the convenience of post-marking at the office. Postage is now generally, and very properly, *pre-paid.*

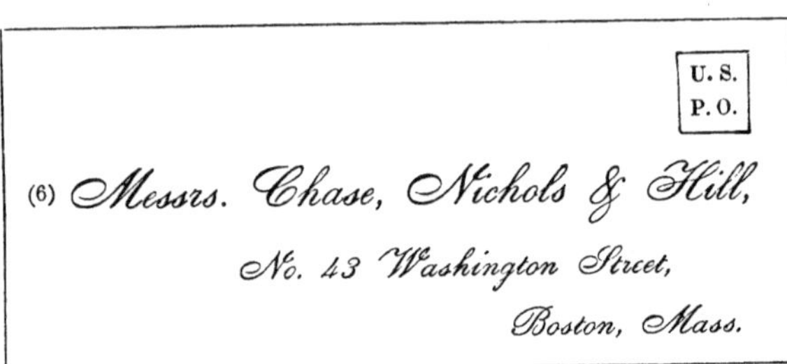

156. The Invoice Book is a book kept by many merchants, into which are *copied* all Invoices, or Bills of Goods purchased. But this requires much labor in copying, and is really of little use; for in case of any difficulty with the seller, it is necessary to refer to *his own list*, and not to a copy of it. Invoices should be carefully compared with the goods actually received, so that in case of disagreement any error may be corrected, and then placed on file for future reference, as occasion shall require. When found correct, they should be entered in the Day Book, to the credit of the person of whom the goods have been received, as in case of credits per Bill. (Arts. 50 and 51.)

157. The Sales Book contains a description of Bills of Merchandise sold. It is kept like the Day Book. When large Bills of Merchandise are sold, the use of the Sales Book enables us greatly to abridge the entry that would otherwise be necessary in the Day Book.

Quest. **155.** What part of the letter or envelope should the superscription occupy? —**156.** What is the Invoice Book? Does this require much labor? Why is it of little use? What should be done with Invoices? When found correct, where should they be entered? —**157.** What is the Sales Book? How is it useful?

BOOKS OF ACCOUNT.

158. Persons are sometimes allowed to introduce their books of account as evidence in their favor; but such testimony is always liable to the strictest scrutiny. A person who would introduce his own books as testimony in his favor in court, must be able to prove, by those who have dealt with him and settled their accounts, that he keeps his books correctly and honestly. He must also be able to prove that the books produced are his account books, and that some of the articles charged have been delivered.

NOTES, ORDERS, AND RECEIPTS.

159. A NOTE is a written or printed paper acknowledging a debt and promising payment. Notes are of different kinds.

160. A PROMISSORY NOTE is a writing which contains a promise to pay money or deliver property to another, at or before a time specified, in consideration of value received by the promisor, or person who signs the note. (The terms *maker* of a note, and *payee* of a note, are defined in Art. 62, which see.)

161. A NEGOTIABLE NOTE is one that may be transferred from one person to another, or that may be bought and sold, and thus have different owners at different times. Notes are usually made payable to the payee or *his order;* to the payee or *bearer;* or simply to *the bearer.* All such notes are *negotiable;* but when a note that has been given to the payee or *his order* is transferred, the payee must *indorse* it by writing his own name upon the back of it. The collec-

QUEST. **158.** Are Books of Account ever received as evidence? To what is such testimony liable? What must a person who would introduce his books as testimony be able to prove?—**159.** What is a Note?—**160.** What is a *Promissory* Note? Who is the *maker*, and who the *payee* of a note?—**161.** What is a *negotiable* note? To whom are notes usually made payable? Are such notes *negotiable?* When must a note be *indorsed?*

tion of a note that is made payable to a specified person, without any mention of *his order* or *the bearer*, can be enforced by the payee only, or by his legal representatives. Such notes are therefore *not* negotiable.

162. A DUE BILL is a written promise to pay a certain sum of money, or a specified amount in goods or property, to a person named, to his order, or to the bearer. Due Bills are notes, though less formal than promissory notes usually are. Whether negotiable or not, depends upon the circumstances just enumerated. (Art. 161.)

163. A BANK NOTE is a promissory note, issued by a banking company, signed by the president and countersigned by the cashier, and payable to the bearer in gold or silver at the bank, on demand. Bank Notes are of course negotiable, being made payable to *the bearer;* and they are usually secured by a deposit of state stocks. (Art. 255.)

164. An ORDER is a written request to deliver money, goods, or other property, to some person specified, to his order, or to the bearer. The person on whom an order may be given is under no legal obligations to pay it, unless he first engages to do so. Orders are generally considered payable on presentation. They are sometimes *accepted* by the person on whom they are drawn. This may be done by his simply writing the word "*Accepted*" either across the back or face of the order, (but usually the latter, and in *red ink*,) and signing his name to it. Before this is done, an order may be regarded as evidence of debt against the *drawer* of it; but afterward, it may be considered as evidence of debt against the *acceptor*, who, in accepting, agrees to pay.

QUEST. **161.** What notes can be collected by the payee only, or by his legal representatives? Are such notes *negotiable?* —**162.** What is a Due Bill? Are due bills notes? — Are they *negotiable?* — **163.** What is a Bank Note? Are bank notes *negotiable?* —**164.** What is an Order? Is the person on whom an order may be drawn under obligations to pay it? When are orders generally considered payable? How may an order be *accepted* by the person upon whom it is drawn? Against whom may an order be considered as evidence of debt?

165. A Receipt is a written statement, signed by the giver of it, acknowledging that he has received a specified amount of money, goods, or other property. A receipt of money may be in part or in full payment of a debt, and it operates as a discharge of the debt either in part or in full, as the case may be. A receipt of goods makes the receiver liable to account for the same, according to the nature of the transaction, or the tenor of the writing. Orders and receipts, like bills of goods, should be preserved and placed on file.

CHECKS, DRAFTS, AND BILLS OF EXCHANGE.

166. Banks are institutions for the deposit and safe keeping of money. (Art. 230.) When merchants and others deposit money in a bank, and keep a bank account, each depositor is usually furnished by the bank with a small Bank Book, on the Cr. side of which are entered his deposits, and on the Dr. side the sums he withdraws. A depositor *has credit* at a bank only while the Cr. side of his account exceeds the Dr. side, unless by special agreement.

167. A Check is an order addressed to a bank for the payment of money to the bearer, to a person named in the check, or to his order. While a depositor has *money to his credit* at a bank, his checks are paid on presentation. But when one's bank account is drawn up, his checks are no longer paid, unless by a special arrangement. Checks should therefore be presented for payment or acceptance as soon after they are given as practicable.

168. A Draft is an order addressed by one bank or mercantile house to another, for the payment of money to a person named, or to his order. When a draft is payable at

Quest. **165.** What is a Receipt? How does a receipt of money operate? How a receipt of goods? What should be done with orders and receipts? — **166.** What are Banks? What is a Bank Book? When has a depositor *credit* at a bank? — **167.** What is a Check? When will a depositor's checks on a bank be paid? When should checks be presented for payment? — **168.** What is a Draft?

sight, or thirty or sixty days after sight, three additional days, known as "days of grace," are by common usage allowed for payment. Drafts are therefore sometimes drawn payable at sight, "without grace." (Form No. 9.)

169. A Bill of Exchange is a written request or order addressed by one bank or commercial house to another, requesting the payment of money to a third person named, or to his order. Bills of Exchange are Domestic and Foreign. When Bills of Exchange are drawn by parties residing in one state or country upon persons in the same state or country, they are called Bills of Domestic Exchange. When the parties to bills reside in different states or countries, and bills which are drawn in one country are made payable in another, they are called Bills of Foreign Exchange.

170. The person who makes or draws and signs a Bill of Exchange is called the *maker* or *drawer;* the person to whom it is addressed, the *drawee,* and the person to whom or to whose order it is payable is called the *payee.* When the drawee accepts a bill he becomes the *acceptor*, and thereby assumes the obligation for its payment according to its tenor. (Art. 164, and Form No. 10.)

171. A Set of Exchange usually embraces three bills of the same date and tenor. When any one of the set is paid the others are void. The object of a Set of Exchange is simply to provide beforehand against inconvenience in case one of the set should be lost in transmission. The holder of a Set of Exchange may send two of the set forward for payment, by different conveyances, and retain the third himself. Then in case one is miscarried the other may reach its destination and be paid. If both are lost the third may be used.

Quest. **168.** What are "days of grace"? How are drafts sometimes made payable? — **169.** What is a Bill of Exchange? What is said of *domestic* exchange, and what of *foreign?* — **170.** Who is the maker or drawer of a bill? Who is the *drawee?* Who the *payee?* Who the *acceptor?* What obligation does the acceptor of a bill assume? — **171.** What is a Set of Exchange? When one of a set is paid, what of the others? What is the object of a set?

No. 1.—*A Promissory Note.*

$45.50. Brooklyn, Sept. 1st, 1860.

Thirty days after date, I promise to pay Samuel Bronson, or Order, at my Store in Brooklyn, Forty-five and $\frac{50}{100}$ Dollars, value received.

Henry Paywell.

No. 2.—*A common Note of Hand.*

$24.00. Washington, September 10th, 1860.

For value received, I promise to pay Ira Merchant, or Bearer, Twenty-four Dollars, the tenth day of July, 1861, with interest from the tenth of January next.

Timothy Truthful.

No. 3.—*A Note for Property.*

$60.00. Whiteford, May 10th, 1860.

Sixty days after date, I promise to deliver to John Burch, or Order, at my Wagon-shop in Whiteford, a good one-horse Wagon worth Sixty Dollars.

Samuel White.

No 4.—*A Due Bill for Goods.*

$14.25. Detroit, June 20th, 1860.

Due Henry Whitcomb, or Order, Fourteen and $\frac{25}{100}$ Dollars in Goods from my Store, value received.

John K. Howard.

No. 5. — *An Order for Money and Goods.*

Monroe, July 25th, 1860.

James Armitage, Esq.

Please pay to William Faithful, or Order, Fourteen Dollars in Goods from your Store, and Six Dollars in money, and charge the same to

$20.00. *Smith & Whitney.*

No. 6. — *A Receipt for Property.*

Received, Whiteford, July 2d, 1860, of Samuel White, a good one-horse Wagon, in full of his agreement of May 10th, 1860. *John Burch.*

No. 7. — *A Receipt in full of all Demands.*

$217.17. *New York, July 10th, 1860.*

Received from James Mitchell, per Job Willson, Two Hundred and Seventeen and $\frac{17}{100}$ Dollars, in full of all demands. *Kingsley & Bingham.*

No. 8. — *A Check, payable to Bearer.*

No. 125. *Albion, Mich., Sept. 10th, 1860.*

Exchange Bank of Albion.

Pay to W. H. Brockway, or Bearer, Three Hundred and Seventy-five and $\frac{25}{100}$ Dollars, and charge the same to the account of

375\frac{25}{100}$ *Samuel Paywell.*

No. 9. — *A Draft, payable to Order.*

No. 237. **Exchange Bank of Albion.**

1225\frac{75}{100}$ *Albion, Mich., Sept. 12th, 1860.*

At sight, without grace, pay to the Order of A. P. Gardner One Thousand Two Hundred and Twenty-five and $\frac{75}{100}$ Dollars, and charge the same to

To The Mercantile Bank, *Mayhew & Irwin.*

New York City.

No. 10. — *A Bill of Exchange.*

Wells, Fargo & Co. EXPRESS AND BANKING OFFICE. *San Francisco, Cal. August 25th, 1860.*

Exchange for $275.00. *No. 182,412.*

At sight of this First of Exchange (Second and Third of same tenor and date unpaid) pay to the Order of J. H. LAPHAM, ESQ., *at your office in Boston, Two Hundred and Seventy-five Dollars, Value received, and charge the same to account of* *Wells, Fargo & Co.*

To Messrs. Wells, Fargo & Co.,
82 Broadway, New York.

No. 10 is a Bill of Exchange drawn by one branch of a Banking House upon another, the same house having several branches. It is drawn in San Francisco, and when indorsed by J. H. Lapham will be paid on presentation at the office in Boston, and charged to the central office in New York. The other two of the set are like this, with but one exception: the words Second and Third alternately take the place of First, which passes within the parenthesis.

QUEST. 171. What is said of Form No. 10? Where is it drawn, and where payable? How do the other bills of the Set of Exchange differ from the first?

PART SECOND.

COMMERCIAL CALCULATIONS.

PERCENTAGE.

172. PERCENTAGE is an allowance made by the hundred. The *number* denoting the allowance is called the *rate* per cent. Thus: 5 per cent. of any number means 5 for every hundred of the number, or 5 hundredths of the number, and is written decimally .05, or 5 %; and so of other rates per cent.

Example 1. What is the percentage of $2565 at 6 per cent.? *Ans.* $153.90.

OPERATION.	
$2565.	*Explanation.* In multiplying the given number by .06, and pointing off as required in decimals, it is evident we obtain 6 hundredths of the number, or 6 per cent. of it;
.06	
$153.90 *Ans.*	

and so of every other number. Hence,

173. To obtain a given percentage of any number. *Multiply the given number by the rate per cent. expressed decimally, and the product will be the percentage.*

Ex. 2. What is 8 per cent. of $450275? *Ans.* $36022.

Ex. 3. What is 4 per cent. of 7850 sheep? *Ans.* 314 sheep.

Ex. 4. What is 17 per cent. of 493 years? *Ans.* 83.81 years.

Ex. 5. What is $1\frac{3}{4}$ per cent. of $8792.80? *Ans.* $153.874.

174. Percentage is applied in various practical concerns in life, among which are Interest, Discount, Exchange, Taxes, Commission, and Insurance.

QUEST. **172.** What is Percentage? What is the *rate* per cent.?—**173.** How do you obtain a given percentage of any number?—**174.** To what is percentage applied?

INTEREST.

175. INTEREST is a sum agreed upon to be paid by the borrower to the lender, for the use of money. It is generally reckoned at a certain *per cent.* by the year; but sometimes at a given *per cent.* by the month.

The PRINCIPAL is the money lent on which interest is paid.

The AMOUNT is the Principal and Interest together.

Example 1. What is the interest of $480 for 2 years, 10 months, and 18 days, at 7 per cent.? What is the amount?

OPERATION.

```
  $480.   Principal.
     .07  Rate.
  ---------
2)33.60   Int. 1 year.
      2   No. of years.
  ---------
  67.20   Int. 2 years.
2)16.80   Int. 6 mos.
3) 8.40   Int. 3 mos.
2) 2.80   Int. 1 mo.
5) 1.40   Int. 15 days.
    .28   Int. 3 days.
  ---------
  96.88   Interest.
 480.     Principal.
  ---------
$576.88   Amount.
```

Explanation. The rate per cent. being 7, it is evident we obtain the interest for 1 year by multiplying by .07; and for 2 years by multiplying the interest for 1 year by 2, the number of years. The interest for 1 year divided by 2 will give the interest for 6 months; and this divided by 2 will give the interest for 3 months, which, divided by 3, will give the interest for 1 month. This last divided by 2 will give the interest for 15 days, which, divided by 5, will give the interest for 3 days. These several sums taken together will give the interest of $480 for 2 years, 10 months, and 18 days. The same principle, it is manifest, will apply to any other sum of money, at any rate per cent., and for any length of time for which we may desire to know the interest. Hence,

176. To find the interest on any given principal, at any rate per cent., and for any length of time, we have the general rule given on the following page.

QUEST. **175.** What is Interest? How is interest reckoned? What is the principal? What the amount? — **176.** How do you find the interest at *any rate* per cent. and for *any length of time*?

GENERAL RULE FOR INTEREST.

I. For Years. *Multiply the principal by the given rate expressed decimally, and the product will be the interest for one year. Then multiply the interest for one year by the number of years for which interest is required.*

II. For Months. *Take such fractional parts of one year's interest as the number of months require.*

III. For Days. *Take such fractional parts of one month's interest as the number of days require.*

Interest. *The interest for the given number of years, months, and days, added together, will be the interest required.*

Amount. *To the interest thus obtained add the principal, and we have the amount.*

Ex. 2. What is the *interest* of $1440 for 5 years, 9 months, and 6 days, at 7 per cent.? *Ans.* $581.28.

Ex. 3. What is the *amount* of $1440 for 3 years, 7 months, and 5 days, at 6 per cent.? *Ans.* $1750.80.

PARTIAL PAYMENTS.

177. When *partial payments* have been made on Notes, Bonds, and written obligations generally, the decisions of the Supreme Court of the United States, and of the Courts of most of the States, recognize the following principles: —

I. *Partial payments apply first in payment of the interest due on an obligation at the time they are made.*

II. *When a payment exceeds the interest due at the time, the excess of payment applies in discharge of the principal. Interests subsequently accruing are to be computed on that part of the principal which remains unpaid, as a* new principal.

III. *When a payment is less than the interest due at the time, the surplus of interest does not augment the principal.*

QUEST. **177.** What principles have been established by the Courts when *partial payments* are made on Bonds and Notes?

Interest in such cases continues on the last principal, *until payments are made which, taken together, exceed the interest due. Any excess of payment at any time, over interests due, applies in discharge of the principal.*

COMPUTATION OF TIME.

178. In computing the time that has elapsed between two different dates, we write the later of the two dates first; then place the earlier date below, and subtract. We write in each instance the year, the number of months that have passed in the year, and the day of the month.*

$1285. NEW YORK, March 8th, 1857.

Ex. 4. For value received I promise to pay Samuel White, or order, Twelve Hundred and Eighty-five Dollars, on demand, with interest at 7 per cent. JAMES MARSHALL.

Partial payments are made on this note as follows:—

Sept. 8, 1857, received	.	$85.50.
June 18, 1858, do.	.	30.25.
March 24, 1859, do.	.	250.00.

What amount was due on taking up the note, Feb. 9, 1860?

Ans. $1166.065.

DISCOUNT.

179. DISCOUNT is an allowance made for the payment of a sum of money before it is due. If I give my note to a man for $107, payable in one year, without interest, the *present worth* of the note is $100; for this sum placed at interest for one year at 7 per cent. will amount to $107 at the time the note becomes due. In this case the *present worth* is $\frac{100}{107}$

* Interest is sometimes computed for a period including both the day on which a note is dated, and the day on which payment is made; or *to the following day*. But time is not thus reckoned in this work.

QUEST. 178. How do you compute the time between two dates?—179. What is Discount? What is the *present worth* of a note for $107, payable in a year, without interest, money being worth 7 per cent.?

or $\frac{1}{1.07}$ of the *face* of the note, or the amount named in it. But $1.07 is the amount of $1. for the time before the note becomes due, with interest at the given rate. Now, the *present worth* of *any* note not drawing interest will sustain a corresponding relation to its *face*, whatever may be the *rate* per cent. at which interest is computed, or the *time* before the note becomes due. Therefore,

180. To find the *present worth* of any sum of money payable at a future time without interest,

Divide the given sum by the amount of $1 *at the given rate and for the given time, and the quotient will be the present worth required.*

181. The *present worth* of a note subtracted from its *face* will give the *true discount.*

BANK DISCOUNT.

182. Bank Discount is the sum charged by Banks for discounting notes and drafts, and is the same as *interest paid in advance,* with this difference: three days are added to the time in computing Bank Discount. But these days are allowed in the payment of notes, and are known as *days of grace.* Therefore,

183. To find the Bank Discount on any Note or Draft payable at a future time, without interest,

Compute the interest on the note or draft for three days more than the time specified, and the result will be the discount required.

184. The *discount* of a bank note subtracted from its *face* gives the present worth of the note, or its *proceeds.*

Quest. **180.** How do you find the *present worth* of a sum due at a future time? —**181.** How do you find the *true discount?*—**182.** What is Bank Discount? What are *days of grace?*—**183.** How do you find the Bank Discount on a note or draft due at a future time without interest?—**184.** How do you find the *proceeds* of such a note?

185. To find the *present worth* by Bank Discount of a note due at a future time, and drawing interest at a given rate per cent.,

Compute the interest on the note to the time it becomes due. The Bank Discount subtracted from the amount of the note when due, will give its present worth.

In case I present an approved note of $100 at the Bank, payable in one year, without interest, and ask to have the same discounted, interest being at 7 per cent. for a year, the officers of the Bank will give me $100, less the interest of $100, or $93. (Art. 182.) The face of the note is therefore $\frac{100}{93}$, or $\frac{1}{.93}$ of the amount of its proceeds, or of its present worth. But $.93 is the present worth of $1.00, by Bank Discount, for the time before the note becomes due, interest being computed at the given rate. Now the proceeds of *any* Bank Note, due at a future time, and not drawing interest, will sustain a corresponding relation to its *face*, whatever may be the *rate* per cent. at which interest is computed, or the *time* before the note becomes due. Therefore,

186. To find the *face* of a Bank Note payable in a specified time, without interest, whose immediate proceeds shall, on discounting the note, amount to a given sum,

Divide the required proceeds by the present worth of $1 at the given rate and for the given time, and the quotient will be the face of the Bank Note required.

EXAMPLES FOR PRACTICE.

Example 1. What is the *true discount* on $407.00 for three months at 7 per cent.? (Arts. 180 and 181.)

Ans. $7.00.

Ex. 2. What is the Bank Discount on $407.00 for three months at 7 per cent.? (Arts. 182 and 183.) *Ans.* $7.36.

QUEST. **185.** How do you find the *present worth*, by Bank Discount, of a note due at a future time and drawing interest at a given rate? How do you find the face of a Bank Note payable in a given time, without interest, whose immediate proceeds shall, on discounting the note, amount to a given sum?

Ex. 3. What is the Bank Discount on $800.00 for thirty days at 7 per cent.? *Ans.* $5.13.

Ex. 4. What is the *true discount* on $800.00 for thirty days at 7 per cent.? *Ans.* $4.64.

Ex. 5. A man has a good note for $800.00, payable at the Exchange Bank the 2d day of September, 1860. It is dated July 2d, 1860, and draws interest at 6 per cent. from date. He procures it discounted at the Bank the 2d day of August, at usual rates with the Bank, legal interest being at 6 per cent. How much money does he receive as the proceeds of his note? *Ans.* $803.556.

Ex. 6. A person wishes to use $1000.00, and can procure money for thirty days at the Bank on his indorsed note at the rate of 7 per cent. per annum. For what amount must his note be drawn that he may realize $1000.00 net proceeds for present use? (Arts. 185 and 186.) *Ans.* $1006.46.

Ex. 7. A person owes a debt of $1500.00, toward the payment of which he is able to raise but $900.00. He offers this sum to be applied in part toward paying the debt, but desires to retain enough to pay in advance the interest due on the balance of the debt, at 8 per cent. per annum, for 9 months, without grace, and secures the same by his indorsed note. What is the face of the note? *Ans.* $638.30.

Ex. 8. A man bought a farm for $4268.00, payable in cash; but as his means are not at present available, he obtains the money for four months at a bank. How large a note is required to raise the money at a discount of 6 per cent. per annum? *Ans.* $4357.325.

EXCHANGE.

187. Exchange, in commerce, implies a mode of paying debts, when debtor and creditor reside in different places, without the actual transmission of money, the indebtedness of the two places to each other being mutually exchanged.

Quest. **187.** What does Exchange imply?

This is done by means of Drafts, or Bills of Exchange, which are usually drawn by one bank upon another. (Arts. 168 to 171, and 234 to 242.)

188. Two Banks in different cities, having confidence in each other, for mutual advantage and the convenience of their customers agree to pay one another's drafts to a given amount. Each bank renders a monthly, weekly, or daily statement of account to the other; and, on settlement, the bank whose drafts upon the other amount to the greater sum pays the balance due in money. This arrangement enables the Banks of two cities to sell Drafts, or Bills of Exchange, upon each other for a less sum than it would cost their customers to send the money from one city to the other, and at the same time to receive enough to pay them for their trouble.

189. The *rate* of Exchange between two places depends upon the character and relative supply of the circulating medium in the two places, and upon the relative indebtedness of the two places to each other. The rate is *higher* when the currency of a place is insufficient in quantity, or poor in quality, and when its relative indebtedness is great. The rate is *lower* when the currency of a place is abundant in quantity, or good in quality, and when its relative indebtedness is small.

190. The *cost* of Exchange to the buyer is generally estimated at a certain rate per cent., and is computed like interest or percentage. Exchange, though sometimes at a discount, generally sells at a premium. Its market value depends, like that of other products, upon the relation of supply and demand. When there is a *large supply* and *little demand,* Exchange is abundant, and consequently *low;* and

---

QUEST. **187.** How is this done? — **188.** What arrangements do Banks make with each other? What does this arrangement enable the Banks to do? — **189.** What does the *rate* of Exchange depend upon? When is the rate *higher*, and when *lower?* — **190.** How is the *cost* of Exchange generally estimated? Does Exchange always sell at a premium? What does its market value depend upon?

sometimes even at a discount. But when the *supply is small* and the *demand great*, Exchange is scarce, and consequently *high*.

EXAMPLES FOR PRACTICE.

Example 1. What is the cost in Chicago of $1260.00 in Exchange on New York, Exchange being at a premium of $2\frac{1}{2}\%$? *Ans.* $1291.50.

Ex. 2. What is the cost in Detroit of $1260.00 in Exchange on New York, Exchange being at a premium of $\frac{3}{4}$ of 1%? *Ans.* $1269.45.

Ex. 3. What is the cost in New Orleans of $1260.00 in Exchange on St. Louis, Exchange being at a *discount* of $\frac{1}{4}$ of 1%? *Ans.* $1256.85.

Ex. 4. What is the cost in New York of $1260.00 in Exchange on Boston, Exchange being at a premium of $\frac{1}{5}$ of 1%? *Ans.* $1262.52.

Ex. 5. What is the cost in Cincinnati of $1260.00 in Exchange on Philadelphia, Exchange being at a premium of $\frac{3}{5}$ of 1%? *Ans.* $1267.56.

Ex. 6. I sell in Detroit $1260.00 in Exchange on St. Louis, at a *discount* of $2\frac{1}{4}\%$, and buy with the proceeds Exchange on Boston at a *premium* of $\frac{3}{4}$ of 1%. What amount in Ex. on Boston do I obtain? *Ans.* $1222.41.

COMMISSION, INSURANCE, AND DUTIES.

191. COMMISSION is an allowance made by a principal to an agent for buying or selling goods, and is generally reckoned at a certain rate per cent.

INSURANCE is security against loss of property by fire, storms, and other casualties, and is known as Fire Insurance, Marine Insurance, or Life Insurance, according to the nature of the indemnity given.

QUEST. **190.** What is the effect of a *large*, and what of a *small* supply? —**191.** What is Commission? How is commission generally reckoned? What is Insurance? Under what names is insurance known?

Duties, in commerce, imply a sum of money which Government requires to be paid on certain imported goods.

192. The principles of Percentage, as already explained and employed in treating upon Interest, Discount, and Exchange, are equally applicable to Commission and Insurance, and to Duties, (except when *specific*,) and need not be further elucidated.

EXAMPLES FOR PRACTICE.

Example 1. I pay an attorney $2\frac{1}{4}\%$ for collecting $760.00. What is his commission? *Ans.* $17.10.

Ex. 2. A merchant pays $1\frac{1}{4}\%$ per annum for insurance on a stock of goods worth $12,500.00. What will he pay for insurance in 2 years? *Ans.* $312.50.

Ex. 3. What are the duties on an invoice of silks purchased in Italy at a cost of $4220.00, the duty being 34% of the invoice? *Ans.* $1434.80.

EQUATION OF PAYMENTS.

193. Equation of Payments is the method of finding the average time of payment of a whole debt, where several sums are due at different times, so that neither party shall sustain loss.

194. To find the average time of payment of a whole debt, where several sums are due at different times,

Multiply each sum by the time before it becomes due. Divide the sum of the products thus obtained by the whole debt, and the quotient will be the average time of payment.

195. This rule is based upon the supposition that the *gain* to a creditor from the payment of a sum of money *before* it becomes due, is equal to the *loss* to him from delay of payment of a like sum for the same length of time *after* it is due;

Quest. **191.** What are Duties? — **192.** What application is made of the principles of Percentage? — **193.** What is Equation of Payments? — **194.** How do you find the average time of payment of a whole debt, when several payments are due at different times? — **195.** Upon what principle is this rule based?

whereas the *gain* is to the *loss* as the *discount* of a given sum is to the *interest* of a like sum for the same time.

ILLUSTRATIVE EXAMPLES.

Example 1. H. Ellis owes me $140, of which $80 falls due in 1 month; $40 in 3 months; and $20 in 4 months. He desires to pay the whole amount at once. In what time shall payment be made so that neither party shall sustain loss? *Ans.* 2 months.

OPERATION.

Am't.	Mos.	Product.
80 ×	1 =	80
40 ×	3 =	120
20 ×	4 =	80
140		280

Explanation. The interest of $80 for 1 month is equal to that of $1 for 80 months. The interest of $40 for 3 mos. is equal to that of $1 for 120 mos. And the interest of $20 for 4 mos. is equal to that of $1 for 80 mos. The whole interest is hence equal to the interest of $1 for 280 mos., (the sum of the products,) which will evidently equal as many months' interest of $140 as 140 is contained times in 280, or 2 mos., which is the time required.

Ex. 2. Sold Merchandise to D. Martin at times and in amounts as stated below. What is the *average date* of all the Bills? *Ans.* May 13th.

Dates and Amts. of Bills.

No. 1,	May 1,	Bill of	$60.
" 2,	" 8,	" "	60.
" 3,	" 16,	" "	60.
" 4,	" 25,	" "	70.

OPERATION.

Am't.	Days.	Product.
60 ×	0 =	00
60 ×	7 =	420
60 ×	15 =	900
70 ×	24 =	1680
250		3000

3000 ÷ 250 = 12 days.

Explanation. We reckon the time from the date of the first Bill, May 1st. The Bills, then, have severally to run as follows: No. 1, 0 days; No. 2, 7 days; No. 3, 15 days; and

QUEST. 195. State and explain the first example in Equation of Payments. State and explain the second example.

No. 4, 24 days. The calculation gives an average of 12 days. As we reckon from May 1st, 12 days added will give the *average date* of the whole, which is May 13th. Hence,

196. To find the *average date* of several bills of various amounts and bearing different dates,

Reckon the time between the earliest date of a bill and the date of each of the several bills, and determine the AVERAGE TIME *of the whole, as in Art.* 194. *This, added to the date from which we reckon, will give the* AVERAGE DATE *required.*

Had the bills in the second example been sold on a credit of 4 or 6 months, the average time of payment for the whole would be the same time after the average date of May 13th, as determined above.

In case bills are sold at various times and on different credits, ascertain when they severally fall due, and then determine the *average time* of payment, as in Art. 194.

Ex. 3. I have an Exchange Mdse. Acct. with Henry Brown. His Debits amount to $800, and their *average date* is June 26th. His Credits amount to $550, and their average date is June 1st. What is the *Balance* of the account, and *when is it due?* *Ans.* $250; due August 21st.

Dr.		Henry Brown							Cr.
June	26	To Mdse.	800	00	June	1	By Mdse.	550	00
					Aug.	21	Balance .	250	00
			800					800	00

OPERATION.

$550 \times 25 = 13{,}750$

$13{,}750 \div 250 = 55$

Explanation. Multiply the smaller side of the account ($550) by the number of days that intervene between

QUEST. 196. How do you find the *average date* of several bills of various amounts and bearing different dates? State and explain the third example.

its date and the date of the larger side, (25;) divide the product (13,750) by the *balance* of the account, ($250,) and the quotient will indicate the *time when the Balance is due,* (55 days,) reckoned from the *date of the larger side* of the account. When the larger side has the *later* date, the time must be *added,* (as in this case;) but when it has the *earlier* date, (as in the next example,) the time must be *subtracted.* In this example my *gain* from the use of $550 the 25 days before June 26th, is equal to my *loss* of the use of $250 (the balance) for 55 days. But 55 days is 1 month and 25 days, which, *added* to June 26th, makes August 21st. (Art. 178.)

Ex. 4. I have an Exchange Mdse. Acct. with Henry Brown. His Debits amount to $800, and their *average date* is June 1st. His Credits amount to $550, and their *average date* is June 26th. What is the *Balance* of the account, and *when is it due?* *Ans.* $250; due April 6th.

Dr.		Henry Brown							Cr.
June	1	To Mdse.	800	00	June	26	By Mdse.	550	00
					April	6	Balance .	250	00
			800	00				800	00

Explanation. This example differs from the third only in the dates. Here the larger side of the account has the earlier date. The computation is made in all respects as in the third example, and with the same result, (55 days.) But as the *larger side* of the account has the *earlier date,* the time must be *subtracted,* or counted back, as stated in the explanation of the last example. In this case my *loss* of the use of $550 the 25 days following June 1st, is equal to the *gain* that

QUEST. **196.** State and explain the fourth example.

would arise from the use of $250 (the balance) for 55 days. But 55 days is 1 month and 25 days, which, *subtracted* from June 1st, leaves April 6th. (Art. 178.) This, then, is the date at which the *balance* was due, and from which interest should be reckoned.

197. These four examples embrace the different cases of averaging accounts that are liable to arise, beginning with the simplest. When an account has only debits or credits, the *average time* is computed as in the second example. When an account has both debits and credits, the *average date* of each is first obtained, as in the second example. This brings the account to the form of the third or fourth example, when it should be treated as these have been.

When an account has debits or credits only, and it is required to determine the *average time* of payment, the process is called Simple Equation; but when an account has both debits and credits, and it is required to determine the time for the payment of the *balance*, the process is called Compound Equation.

Equation of Payments, both Simple and Compound, may be computed by *interest*, which some prefer. To do this, we compute the *interest* on the several sums for the length of time we have used as a multiplier, and then ascertain how long it will take the *sum total*, or the required *balance*, as the case may be, *to earn the same interest.* The results are the same, whichever method we employ.

Ex. 5. Sold Joseph Sterling Merchandise at four different times, in amounts as stated in the following Account Current. The first three bills are at a credit of 4 months, and the fourth

QUEST. **197.** What do the four examples given in Equation of Payments embrace? How do you obtain the *average time* when an account has only debits or credits? How do you obtain the average time for the payment of a *balance*, when an account has both *debits* and *credits?* When is the equation of payments called *simple*, and when *compound?* May equation of payments be computed by *interest?* How? Are the results the same in both cases? What does the Account Current in the fifth example show?

is at a credit of 3 months. Two Cash payments were made, together amounting to $880.00, which are credited.

Dr.		Joseph Sterling								Cr.
Jan.	16	Mdse. 4 mo.	560	00	Mar.	25	Cash	450	00
Feb.	1	" 4 "	380	00	May	20	"	430	00
"	16	" 4 "	340	00	April	22	Average	880	00
Apr.	21	" 3 "	400	00	Aug.	5	Balance	800	00
June	11	Average . .	1680	00				1680	00

Required to Determine:

1st. What is the *average date* at which these four Bills become due? *Ans.* June 11th.

2d. What is the *average date* of the two Cash payments, together amounting to $880.00? *Ans.* April 22d.

3d. When will the *Balance* of the account ($800.00) become due by Equation? *Ans.* August 5th.

The answers to these several questions are entered in the Account Current in Roman type; but the learner should determine them for himself, and seek to acquire the mastery of all the principles here involved.

When an Account Current embraces a period of several months, and contains a large number of small items, the sums falling due in any one month are frequently added, and the amount treated as though falling due the middle of the month, or the first of the following month. Absolute accuracy is in this manner closely approximated, and much labor is at the same time saved in the computation.

QUEST. 197. What three things is it required to determine? What is done when an Account Current embraces a period of several months, and contains a large number of items? Is the labor thus saved at the expense of accuracy?

STORAGE, DIVIDENDS, AND LOSSES.

198. The EQUATION OF STORAGE, the EQUATION OF DIVIDENDS, and the ADJUSTMENT OF LOSSES, are all determined by the application of a like principle to that already stated for the *Equation of Payments.* (Art. 194.)

PARTNERSHIPS.

199. PARTNERSHIP is the associating of two or more persons for the transaction of business, with an agreement to share, according to contract, the profits and losses arising therefrom. Partnerships are *simple* and *compound.*

200. A SIMPLE PARTNERSHIP is when the stock of different partners is employed in business an equal length of time. To find each partner's share of the gain or loss, say,

As the whole stock is to each partner's stock, so is the whole gain or loss to each partner's share of the gain or loss.

201. A COMPOUND PARTNERSHIP is when the stock of different partners is employed in business unequal lengths of time. To find each one's share of the gain or loss,

Multiply each partner's stock by the time it has been employed in business; then say, As the sum of the products is to each product, so is the whole gain or loss to each partner's share of the gain or loss.

Example. A and B engage in business for two years, and agree to share their gains according to their stock in trade. A at first puts in $5000.00, and at the end of four months adds $2000.00. B at first puts in $8000.00, but at the end of six months withdraws $3000.00. They gain $2980.00. What is each one's share of the gain?

Ans. A's share $1600.00; B's share $1380.00.

QUEST. **198.** What is said of Equation of Storage, Dividends, and Losses? — **199.** What is Partnership? How divided? — **200.** What is a *simple* partnership? How do you find each partner's share of the gain or loss? — **201.** What is *compound* partnership? How do you find each partner's share in the gain or loss in *compound* partnership?

PART THIRD.

PHILOSOPHY AND MORALS OF BUSINESS.

CHOICE OF BUSINESS.

ART. **202.** Scores of young men, and many a young woman, in nearly every township and village of our country, are considering for themselves, and proposing to one another for solution, questions like these: What shall I turn my attention to for a business for life? What can I best do for a living? And having selected an employment, they inquire: What are the legitimate sources of gain open to me in my chosen pursuit? How can I honestly prosecute my business so as most certainly to insure success? These and like questions will here be examined, with the hope of presenting considerations that shall aid in establishing rational plans for successful business.

203. Human beings in *solitude*, cut off from all social relations, may freely employ their faculties as they choose, being responsible only to their Creator for the use they make of them. But when several persons associate together for mutual pleasure and benefit, they, in the nature of the case, do so on the ground of *equality of rights.* All appetites, passions, and desires, which persons may properly indulge in *solitude*, may with equal propriety be gratified in *society;* but only in such a manner as not to interfere with the equal rights of others.

QUEST. **202.** What questions in relation to the choice of a business are often asked? What is the object of considering such questions here? — **203.** What freedom may persons in solitude exercise? Upon what basis do associations for mutual pleasure and benefit rest? What gratifications may persons seek in society, and with what restriction?

204. The law of *reciprocity*, which lies at the very foundation of civil society, recognizes this *equality of rights*, and requires that each person shall leave every other one in the unrestrained possession of that liberty which he desires for himself; and that all shall unite together for the protection of each in the enjoyment of his natural rights. The teachings of this law none may disregard.

205. But in the formation of a society where each person is acquainted with the law of reciprocity, and where each is disposed to obey this law, no one will be required to surrender any thing without himself deriving advantage therefrom. None, hence, can become *losers* in the formation of a society based upon such principles. On the contrary, each will be a *gainer*. Alone, each is weak, and unable to defend himself in the enjoyment of his rights. Society hence undertakes to protect individuals in the enjoyment of their rights, and to redress wrongs as they may occur. This, society has a right to do; for each individual is supposed to promise obedience to the law of reciprocity, which is a law of his nature, and which is essential to the existence of civil society.

206. In accordance with these principles, it is apparent that each individual is, and of right ought to be, at liberty to select any employment which he may pursue with advantage to himself and with benefit to the community in which he lives. But if any person determines upon an employment, the practice of which works ill to his neighbor, he thereby forfeits his claim upon society for protection in its pursuit, inasmuch as he disregards the law which underlies the formation of civil society, and which is essential not only to its proper maintenance but to its very existence. Such a one can have

QUEST. **204.** What is said of the law of *reciprocity?* — **205.** What is said of a society based upon the law of reciprocity? Who are *losers*, and who *gainers* in such a society? What of persons *alone?* What protection does society afford? Why may society *protect rights* and *redress wrongs?* — **206.** What kind of employments may persons select? When does any one forfeit his claim upon society for protection in a pursuit, and why?

no claim for any thing better than solitude, and the life of a hermit, till he can yield cheerful obedience to the requirements of reciprocity. (Arts. 203 to 205.)

207. In application of these principles it is manifest that any person may properly raise corn, wheat, and potatoes, which are good for food. He may build houses and barns, make wagons and farm implements, and engage in kindred useful employments. He may erect flouring mills, and buy wheat at a fair price, and manufacture and sell flour at a reasonable advance. He may in like manner raise stock, and make butter and cheese. He may sell wool to be manufactured into clothing, and hides to be made into leather, and this into boots and shoes. He may further buy the surplus products of the country, which are not required at home, and exchange them for the manufactures and products of others, which his neighbors need; for all this can be done to the mutual advantage of all parties affected by these several transactions. These and other similar pursuits may be prosecuted in harmony with the requirement that we "do unto others as we would that others should do unto us."

208. But highway robbery, theft, forgery, gambling in all its forms, and all kindred employments, are in clear violation of the law of reciprocity. (Art. 204.) Their pursuit is subversive of right and justice, and of every principle that underlies and permeates well-regulated communities. Civil society, through its constituted authorities, should hence seek to free itself from all such modes of disturbing the public peace and jeoparding the public weal, and in all suitable ways discourage minor wrongs generally, and every form of employment that tends to idleness and dissipation, while at the same time it should aim to encourage employments that are

QUEST. **206.** What claim, only, has he? — **207.** Apply these principles to various proper employments. — **208.** What employments are in violation of the law of reciprocity? What should society do with reference to them? What employments should society encourage?

right and proper, and the pursuit of which will best promote the general good of the entire community.

LABOR THE SOURCE OF WEALTH.

209. The Creator, who made man with physical and intellectual faculties adapted to labor, has wisely ordered that labor is necessary in order to obtain the comforts and conveniences of life, no less than as a means of preserving and improving physical and mental health. But the laborer has his reward; for he alone is entitled to the fruits of his industry. While he regards the rights of his neighbor he may gain all he can, and use what he gains as he will. This is the reason why human labor in different countries is commonly exerted in proportion as the rights of property are understood and enforced.

210. We hence see the wisdom of maintaining correct systems of popular education; of every where teaching respect to the rights of property; and of inculcating obedience to the law of reciprocity. We hence also see the reason why moral and religious nations increase in wealth, while the vicious and irreligious struggle with poverty.

211. While labor is the source of wealth, it is also true that industry in some pursuits is more productive than in others, and that the aptitudes of men for different pursuits are very dissimilar. It therefore becomes each person to devote himself to an employment for which he has an aptitude, and in the pursuit of which he may derive satisfaction and attain success.

212. *Simple labor*, which is all that is requisite in order to produce the *necessaries* of life, requires only the exercise

QUEST. **209.** What is said of the necessity for labor? What reward has the laborer? What may he gain, and how use his gains? How is labor exerted in different countries? — **210.** What of education? What nations increase in wealth, and what remain poor? — **211.** What is remarked of industry in different pursuits, and of the aptitudes of men? What should each person hence do?

of such skill as may be readily acquired by persons generally. The simplest forms of labor require little more than the exercise of *physical force*, and are hence remunerated at the *lowest wages*. In proportion as *skill* is associated with labor will *wages advance*. This is because skill is more rare than physical force, and requires *education* and *practice*.

213. Beyond this, wages are affected by the degree of *confidence* which may safely be reposed in the laborer; or, in other words, by his *moral character*. It is hence appropriate for each one to devote himself to the highest form of industry for which he has an aptitude, and in which he can attain the necessary skill and trustworthiness, provided there is a demand for such labor where he resides. At all events, every one should *do something*, and *do it well*. All useful labor is honorable. Each should render to society, in such form as he is able, an equivalent for the benefits he receives. This justice requires. The apostle accordingly commanded, *If any man will not work, neither let him eat.*

HOW TO RENDER LABOR MOST PRODUCTIVE.

214. We have seen that *labor* is the source of wealth, and that *wages* are affected by the skill of the laborer, and by the degree of confidence that may be reposed in him. Beyond this we remark that the productiveness of labor is increased by its association with *capital*. The following illustration will show how *capital*, *skill*, and *trustworthiness* severally and conjointly render labor more productive.

215. While half a dozen men, with their unassisted hands, would be engaged in constructing a *rude hut*, hardly fit for

QUEST. **212.** What say you of the skill necessary for the performance of *simple labor*, and of the wages it will command? How does *skill* affect wages? Why is this? —**213.** Are wages affected by the *character* of the laborer? To what form of industry may each devote himself? What should every one do? What say you of all useful labor? What should each person render to society? What said the apostle of him who will not work? —**214.** What has been remarked of *labor*, and *wages*? What effect has *capital* upon the productiveness of labor?

the occupancy of savages, give each of them an *ax*, and they will in the same time make a comfortable *log house.* Give them the benefit of a *saw mill,* with suitable tools, and the *skill* necessary for their profitable use, and they will erect a commodious *dwelling house,* befitting a civilized state of society. One man with an *ax* and a *team* can gather more wood for fuel in a single day, than twenty men could with their unassisted hands in a week.

216. He who has the full exercise of his physical powers, but is without skill in any trade or business, can engage only in the *simplest forms of labor,* and as a consequence will receive *low wages.* But let a man unite with his labor *skill* in some useful trade, as that of a carpenter, a mason, a wagon-maker or a blacksmith, and his services will command higher wages. Unite with labor and skill that *trustworthiness* which qualifies a man for the care of a manufactory, of a flouring mill, of a merchant's counting-room, or of any important business, and his services, being more valuable to his employer, will be remunerated at a higher rate.

217. Skill and trustworthiness render labor more productive and more desirable, in agriculture, in the mechanic arts, in merchandise, in commercial pursuits generally, and in every branch of productive industry. It therefore becomes each individual, on selecting an employment, to attain in it that *skill,* and to bring to it that *fidelity,* which shall render his services most desirable to his employer. These will enable him to command higher wages while working for others; and in case he desires to engage in business on his own account, they will enable him to procure any assistance he may need, on the most advantageous terms.

QUEST. **215.** Show the value of an *ax*, and of a *saw mill*, with tools and *skill* in their use. Show the value of an *ax* and a *team.*—**216.** What of the wages of *labor* without *skill?* What effect has *skill* upon wages? What is the effect upon wages when the laborer unites with his skill *trustworthiness?*—**217.** What forms of labor do skill and trustworthiness benefit? On selecting an employment what should each person do? In what ways will *skill* and *fidelity* benefit their possessor?

BENEFITS FROM EXCHANGES.

218. Were every man to labor in that pursuit for which he has the greatest aptitude, each would be engaged in the production of *one*, or at most of but a *few things*, while the innocent gratification of his desires would require the possession and use of a *thousand products*. The truth of this proposition, and the benefits resulting from a division of labor, and from exchanges, may be easily illustrated.

219. The manufacturer of *brooms* might be able to supply a thousand families with the product of his industry, while he requires but one broom for his own use, and yet himself be destitute of *bread;* while the farmer might raise *bread stuffs* enough to supply a hundred families, and still himself be destitute of a broom. The same might be true of the boot and shoe maker, of the chair maker, of the blacksmith, of the wagon maker, and of a score of persons engaged in different pursuits. Such considerations as these create the necessity for exchanges, by which men are enabled to dispose of their surplus products, which they can not themselves use, and receive therefor the products of others, which they have not, but which they need.

220. Each person, by thus producing that in which he is well skilled, and for which he has the greatest aptitude, and by exchanging the same with others who have also a surplus of their own products, is enabled to derive enjoyment from the possession and use of a thousand productions, and is consequently happier than he would otherwise be. And as the same is true of *all persons*, we can see the advantage that would result to each and to all — to individuals and to communities — from a division of labor and from exchanges.

QUEST. **218.** What would be the result were every man to labor in that pursuit for which he has the greatest aptitude? — **219.** Illustrate the benefits derivable from exchanges. — **220.** Show the influence of a division of labor and of exchanges upon the well being and happiness of persons and communities.

221. In fixing the exchangeable value of products, the desirableness of the employment, the amount of labor, and the degree of skill which are required in their production, must be taken into the account.

HOW MERCHANTS ARE USEFUL.

222. It is desirable to effect these exchanges with all practicable economy; and the more rapidly they are made the better for all. It is from this consideration that *merchants* become necessary in facilitating *exchanges.* The merchant receives from each of his customers their surplus products, which they can not themselves use, and is thus enabled, by exchange in kind, to supply the wants of others. He is in this manner enabled to conduct the exchanges for a whole neighborhood more perfectly, and at less expense of time and labor, than though each producer were to conduct his own exchanges without the merchant's aid.

223. Intelligence and skill are essential to constitute a succesful merchant, for they enable him to seek from one class of his customers what he knows another class need, and to receive from these such products as will be required by others. It is thus that the merchant is enabled to make the exchanges which his customers require, more cheaply than they could do it among themselves without his agency, and still receive from each enough to compensate him for his skill and labor, and for the use of his capital.

224. The principle is the same with different nations, when each is enabled to produce an excess of one class of productions which are desired by the other. The wholesale merchant buys the surplus products of his own country,

QUEST. **221.** What circumstances must be taken into the account in fixing the exchangeable value of products? — **222.** What is remarked of the cost of exchanges, and of the rapidity with which they are made? Show how merchants are useful in effecting exchanges in kind. — **223.** Of what advantage are intelligence and skill to the merchant? How are his customers benefited by the merchant's intelligence and skill? — **224.** When may nations be benefited by exchanges?

where they are not needed, and exchanges them with the merchant of another country, where they are desired, for their surplus products, which can not be raised in his own country, but which his customers nevertheless need. The people of each country are thus enabled to gratify more innocent desires, and are consequently happier than they were before.

225. In exchanges which are conducted on the principle here stated, each party is benefited. And the most favorable commerce to any country is that which enriches all countries affected by it most rapidly. It is with nations as with individuals engaged in commerce: each derives the greatest benefit to itself while most industriously and successfully laboring to supply the wants of the other. So intimately are the interests of each united with the welfare of others, that a bargain should never be made unless both parties to it can be gainers thereby. This principle applies to single persons, to separate communities, and to different nations.

HOW MONEY FACILITATES EXCHANGES.

226. When we have any work to be done it is desirable to effect it in the best manner possible, and at the least expense practicable. This is the reason why we use a wagon for transporting merchandise, and for carrying the products of the farm to market in summer and autumn, and a sleigh in winter; and why we employ a steamboat, a vessel, or a rail car, in preference to either sleigh or wagon, when practicable.

227. We have already seen that the services of the merchant enable us to effect exchanges more rapidly and more economically than could otherwise be done. (Arts. 222 to 225.) But it frequently happens that persons desire to sell more or less, in value, of their products, than they wish, at the

QUEST. **224.** How are such exchanges effected? How do they influence national happiness? — **225.** Who are benefited by such exchanges? What is the most favorable commerce to any country? When only should a bargain be made? — **226.** How is it desirable to do any kind of work? Illustrate.

time, to receive in return of the products of others. Moreover, they often want to sell their own products without purchasing any thing in return. So, likewise, they frequently desire to purchase the products of others when they have none of their own to dispose of. To meet such necessities some object of *universal desire* has been found needful.

228. As a means of adjusting such differences, and of facilitating exchanges, the nations of the earth, generally, have agreed upon a *metallic currency* as this object of universal desire. It is because the precious metals have been found the most convenient instrument in effecting exchanges that they have been so universally employed for this purpose. But for this circumstance, oranges, or precious stones, or some other instrument, might as well have been used as they. (Arts. 252 to 257.)

229. The money of civilized nations generally, consists of *silver* and *gold;* or of these and a paper currency, which is adopted from economy and convenience, and which is redeemable in the precious metals. Every person having any thing to sell is willing to dispose of it for silver and gold, (or their representative;) for he knows that with these he can procure any thing he desires.

OF BANKS AND BANKING.

230. Banks were originally designed as institutions for the deposit and safe keeping of money. They are of three kinds: (1.) Banks of Deposit; (2.) Banks of Discount; and, (3.) Banks of Circulation. Two of these functions, and not unfrequently all three of them, are performed by the same institution, and with advantage, as we shall presently see.

QUEST. **227.** Why is some object of *universal desire* necessary in effecting exchanges? — **228.** What has been agreed upon as this object of universal desire? Why have the precious metals been employed in effecting exchanges? — **229.** Of what does the money of civilized nations generally consist? Why are persons willing to sell their surplus products for silver and gold? — **230.** What was the original design of banks? Of how many kinds are banks, and what are they?

231. There is also another classification of banks having reference both to the authority from which they derive their origin and powers, and to the functions they perform. The second arrangement is likewise into three classes, namely: (1.) Commercial Banks; (2.) State Banks; and, (3.) Private Banks.

BANKS OF DEPOSIT.

232. Banks of Deposit are useful for the safe keeping of money. The precious metals are small in bulk, and are therefore very liable to be stolen. The coins of the same denomination being made precisely alike, can not be identified in case they are stolen. Great care is hence necessary to protect them. The security of each person against robbery requires that his money be kept in a safe. Otherwise house-breaking and highway robbery would become frequent. But one trusty person, with a good safe, may serve as banker for a neighborhood or village, and at less expense keep the money of twenty merchants with greater safety than each could keep his own.

233. This method of keeping the money of a neighborhood or village has several advantages. The banker opens an account with each merchant and person depositing money with him. He credits each one for the amount he deposits, and debits him for the sums he withdraws. Each individual having money on deposit is at liberty to draw it out in person, as he may need it for use; or he may give a check on the banker requesting him to pay it to another person who may himself have an account at the bank.

234. Suppose A, who has money deposited in a bank, wishes to pay B five hundred dollars. His easiest way to do it is to give B a check on the bank for this sum. If B

QUEST. **231.** Into how many classes is the second arrangement of banks, and what are they? — **232.** How are Banks of Deposit useful? State at length how they are useful. — **233.** How are accounts kept at banks? How may persons having money on deposit use it? — **234.** State how several persons who keep their accounts at the same bank may most conveniently pay and receive money.

does not require the money for use at the time, on presenting his check at the bank the banker will charge A five hundred dollars, and credit B the same amount. If B wishes to pay C five hundred dollars he will do it in the same way. C might wish to pay D, and D might owe A the same amount, and both would make payment in like manner. At the close of the day each man's bank account would stand as it was in the morning; and yet each of these four persons has received five hundred dollars, and each has paid out five hundred dollars. A few entries in the books of the bank thus save the handling and counting of four thousand dollars, the wear of coin, the liability to loss, and the temptation, from exposure, to theft and robbery.

235. The case will be essentially the same with each of twenty merchants who keep their accounts at the same bank; for it is evident that every merchant will, on the whole, buy as much as he sells, and sell as much as he buys. He will, therefore, not only have occasion to deposit as much money as he withdraws, but in any given time he will withdraw nearly the amount he deposits.

236. And what is true of four men or twenty merchants for a day or a week, will be true of all men in the community for all time. And what is true of one bank will be true of any number of banks that are required for the transaction of the business of a city; for at the close of each day, banks holding checks upon each other that have been deposited with them by their customers, exchange these checks, the bank that holds the least amount in checks or drafts upon the other paying the difference in money.

237. Banks of Deposit generally unite with them the functions of Banks of Exchange, to the mutual advantage of

QUEST. **234.** What is thus saved by a few entries in the books of a bank? — **235.** Will the same be true of a greater number of persons, and why? — **236.** Show how the same is true of any number of persons, and of different banks in the same city. — **237.** What other functions do Banks of Deposit perform, and to whose benefit?

their customers and themselves, as we shall presently see. (Arts. 238 to 242.)

238. It is manifest that cities and states, as well as individuals and merchants, will, on the whole, buy as much as they sell, and sell as much as they buy. If Detroit, for example, buys one hundred thousand dollars' worth of merchandise of New York, Detroit must send one hundred thousand dollars' worth of products with which to pay for it; or each city must pay for its purchases of the other in money. If Detroit pays New York money for goods, it is apparent that New York must pay Detroit money in return for products received. This will require that the goods and products purchased of one another by these two cities, *and the money paid for them*, be both transported from each city to the other at every exchange, which would involve great expense, delay, and hazard. (Art. 232.)

239. All this inconvenience may be avoided by the agency of banks in these two cities. Let us suppose that A, in Detroit, sells ten thousand dollars' worth of flour to B, of New York. Instead of counting the specie, and being at the expense and risk of conveying it to Detroit, it is evident A may draw on B for the amount, to be paid to whomsoever A shall direct. And suppose again that C, in New York, sells ten thousand dollars' worth of merchandise to D, of Detroit. It is plain that C is entitled, in like manner, to draw on D for this amount. Now A, of Detroit, who has ten thousand dollars due him in New York, may make his draft on B for this amount, and deposit it to his own credit in the Detroit Bank, through which he does his business. In like manner, C, of New York, who has ten thousand dollars due him in Detroit, may make his draft on D for the same amount,

QUEST. **238.** What is remarked of the purchases and sales of cities and states? Give an illustration, and state the manner of payment. — **239.** Through what agency may the payment of money from one city to another be most easily made? State at length how payment may be made by the agency of banks, in case of purchases and sales between persons residing in different cities, as Detroit and New York.

and deposit it to his credit in the New York Bank, through which he transacts his business. In this way A, of Detroit, and C, of New York, obtain each a credit of ten thousand dollars in his own bank. Each credit is based on a draft upon a person residing in the other city, the payment of which the drawer guarantees. The two banks exchange these drafts by mail, each debiting the other for the draft sent, and each crediting the other for the draft received. Now, each bank charges ten thousand dollars to its own depositor to cover the draft it holds, each bank retaining the draft thus charged as its voucher on settlement with its depositor. In this manner the *indebtedness* of persons in each of these two cities, to persons in the other city, is *exchanged;* and the frequent transmission of large amounts of money is thus saved. Now, all this costs but a few cents postage, and a few entries in the books of each bank; and there is thus saved the time, the cost, and the risk of transporting twenty thousand dollars between these two cities. It is evident that these banks, beside their own compensation for services thus rendered, will by this means be enabled to save a considerable amount to their customers.

240. What we have supposed true of four persons residing in these two cities must be essentially true of any number of persons residing in commercial centers in different states, or in foreign countries. There may be this difference. One state or city may buy of another more or less than it sells to it in return. In such cases the party making the largest purchases must sell enough to other states and cities to make up the difference. Whenever the trade between two cities is unequal, that whose sales to the other are least, must make up the difference in drafts upon other cities or states to which it makes sales, or by payment in money.

QUEST. **239.** What is the actual cost of this mode of payment, and what is saved by it? —**240.** Is the same principle of general application? What difference may there be, and how must it be made up? What of inequality of trade between cities generally, and how is the difference made up?

241. If Michigan, for example, buys more merchandise of New York than New York desires of the products of Michigan in payment, the difference may be made up by sales of the products of Michigan to New England, and the balance due to New York may be paid in the drafts of Michigan on New England. Any difference arising in this or any other way, it is plain can be made up by sending specie, or bank notes redeemable in specie, to the city or country whose sales are the largest, in such amounts as shall be necessary to make up the deficiency. In such cases the equilibrium can be restored through the agency of Banks of Exchange, with greater expedition, economy, and safety, than by individual dealers without the aid of banks.

242. It is manifest that the principles just elucidated will apply with like effect in equalizing exchanges between Chicago and Boston, Cincinnati and Philadelphia, New Orleans and St. Louis; or between any two of these cities, and between all cities and countries however remote from each other.

BANKS OF DISCOUNT.

243. All production results, as we have seen, from the application of industry to capital. (Art. 209.) Now the closer the connection between industry and capital, the more rapid will be the increase in production. But some men have industry and skill, without capital, and must hence labor, if at all, for others; while other men have capital, but from age, or circumstances in life, have not the industry and skill which are required to be united with it in order to render it productive. It is manifest that, in such cases, both parties may be benefited by an equitable arrangement for uniting

QUEST. **241.** When the trade between Michigan and New York is unequal, how may the difference be made up? How may any difference *always* be made up? Are banks in such cases serviceable? — **242.** Of how general application are these principles? — **243.** Of what is production the result? When one person has industry and skill, and another has capital, how may both parties be benefited?

the industry and skill of the former with the capital of the latter. But how shall this union be accomplished?

244. Now, Banks of Discount offer facilities for bringing together borrower and lender, and for the union of the industry and skill of the one, with the capital of the other, in such a manner as shall be most advantageous to each. Banks are enabled to perform this office on much the same principle that gives merchants the ability to serve the community in facilitating exchanges. (Arts. 222 to 225.)

245. Persons who have money which they wish to lend, associate themselves together and establish a bank, at which others apply, who wish to borrow. The stockholders appoint a president and cashier, and elect the necessary directors to superintend the business of the bank. These officers devote their attention to the safe and advantageous loaning of money, and to looking after the varied interests of the bank, without requiring the constant attention of the stockholders generally, who are thus left at liberty to engage in other pursuits.

246. While banks are thus taking care of their own money, they are enabled often to serve their neighbors in the safe-keeping of any moneys they possess, which they do not wish for the time to employ in business themselves, while at the same time the banks may derive sufficient advantage from the use of such moneys to compensate them for their trouble. It will readily be seen that such an arrangement affords greater facilities for the constant union of labor with capital, and for the increased productiveness of a country, than would otherwise exist. While banks are thus beneficial to the whole community, they will be especially advantageous to both borrower and lender.

QUEST. **244.** For what do Banks of Discount offer facilities? How are banks enabled to perform this service? — **245.** How are banks organized, and what officers are employed? — **246.** How may banks be serviceable to their neighbors in the safe-keeping of moneys? How are banks compensated for the care of such moneys? How do such arrangements affect the union of labor with capital? To whom, then, are banks beneficial, and to whom are they especially advantageous?

247. SAVINGS BANKS, which are of recent origin, deserve to be mentioned in this connection. While Banks of Discount generally and properly decline to pay interest on moneys deposited with them, and subject to withdrawal at any time, and dislike to receive small sums on deposit at all, it is the design of Savings Banks to afford those who have any thing to spare, though in small amounts, an opportunity to deposit their *savings* in safety, and to receive *interest* for sums deposited from time to time, by which means they provide against seasons of sickness and distress, and insure a competency for age. This can be done, when moneys so deposited are not subject to be withdrawn without timely notice, and still pay a *few* responsible persons for the care of the savings of the *many* who deposit in them.

248. Savings Banks, which were first established in Great Britain in the early part of the present century, have been rapidly introduced into most civilized countries, and with great advantage to that class of persons for whose benefit they were established. They also benefit the prudent borrower, and the whole community; for while they encourage industry, temperance, and frugality, with the poorer classes, they at the same time serve more closely to unite the entire capital and industry of the country. (Arts. 214 to 217.)

BANKS OF CIRCULATION.

249. While Banks of Circulation usually perform the functions of Banks of Deposit, of Exchange, and of Discount, as we have already considered them, they add thereto the feature of issuing their own notes for *circulation* as *money*, which notes are redeemable in specie on presentation at the bank.

QUEST. **247.** Do banks generally pay *interest* on deposits subject to withdrawal? Do they like to receive *small sums* on deposit? What is the design of Savings Banks? When can interest be safely allowed on deposits? — **248.** When and where were Savings Banks first established? Into what countries have they been introduced? Who are benefited by savings banks, and how? — **249.** What functions do **Banks** of Circulation perform?

250. The Bank of Venice, which was established in 1171, was a Bank of Deposit only. The Bank of Amsterdam, which was established in 1609, and the Bank of Hamburg, established in 1619, were both Banks of Deposit and Exchange. The Bank of England, established in 1694, the Bank of France, established in 1716, and the Banks of the United States, chartered in 1791 and in 1816, were all Banks of Deposit and Exchange, and of Discount and Circulation.

251. Banks during the present century have become more numerous, and have generally owed their existence to special acts of the State Legislatures where they have been located. But Free Banking Laws are now in operation in several of the states, under general laws and regulations, calculated alike to benefit and protect both the banks and the bill holders, and at the same time to subserve the interests of the entire community among whom the bills circulate. (Arts. 255 to 257.)

QUALITY AND FUNCTIONS OF MONEY.

252. Money, as we have seen, is an instrument for facilitating exchanges. (Arts. 226 to 229.) This it does by furnishing an object of *universal desire* to produce an equilibrium where exchanges in kind are unequal.

253. That is the best instrument for effecting exchanges which enables us to accomplish the object in the shortest time, with the greatest ease, and at the least expense. A metallic currency, consisting of silver and gold, has by common consent been agreed upon as this instrument. There are several circumstances which contribute to render it a

QUEST. **250.** What is remarked of the earlier banks, and when were they established? — **251.** What of banks during the present century? What is said of Free Banks? Under what regulations are free banks established, and whose interests are subserved by them? — **252.** What is money? How does money facilitate exchanges? — **253.** What is the best instrument for effecting exchanges? What has been agreed upon as this instrument? What circumstances render silver and gold a desirable instrument for effecting exchanges?

desirable instrument for this purpose, among which are the following. (1.) The labor necessary to its production is but slightly variable at different times and in different places. (2.) A small bulk represents great value, or a large amount of labor in its production. (3.) The precious metals are susceptible of division without loss of value. (4.) They are easily verified, and their great weight affords a ready means for the detection of adulteration. (5.) They are slightly liable to decay, or to diminution in value, except by wear; and, (6.) Being of different values, *silver* may be employed for coins of the lower denominations, and *gold* for the higher. All of these circumstances conspire to render the precious metals a desirable instrument for facilitating exchanges.

254. Government lends its aid in further rendering silver and gold a desirable instrument for conducting exchanges. This it does by regulating the *purity*, the *size*, and the *form* of different coins, so as to render them most safe and convenient for general use, and by causing the work of coining to be done in the best manner possible, and at the least expense, so as most effectually to guard against counterfeiting. We will now see how banks are further useful in facilitating exchanges. (Arts. 232 to 242, and 255 to 264.)

255. Banks are generally and properly required by their charters, or the laws authorizing their establishment, to deposit state stocks, or other good and reliable securities, with the state treasurer, in sufficient amount to insure the payment of all bills they are authorized to issue. As a further protection against loss to bill holders from fraud or otherwise, the bills issued are required to bear the signature of a state register. When good and sufficient securities are thus given, the holders of bank bills are well protected against loss; for

---

QUEST. **254.** Does Government aid in rendering silver and gold a desirable instrument for conducting exchanges? What does government regulate, and with what advantage to the public? — **255.** What security are banks required to give for the redemption of their bills? Why are bank bills required to be countersigned by a state register? Show how bill holders are protected against loss from bank failures.

in case the banks fail to pay their notes, the state has the means of their redemption in the stocks deposited.

256. Where bank notes are redeemable in specie on presentation at the banks issuing them, it is apparent that holders prefer the notes to the specie; otherwise they would go to the banks and exchange the notes for the specie.

257. Bank notes, redeemable in specie on presentation at the bank, possess the following advantages over specie. (1.) While they answer equally well as an instrument in effecting exchanges, they possess less intrinsic value. (2.) The wear and tear from their use is less than that of silver and gold. (3.) They are more easily counted, and more cheaply and more conveniently transported. (4.) They occupy less space, and attract less notice, and are hence less liable to be stolen; and, (5.) If stolen, they are more easily identified than specie, and may hence be more readily recovered.

258. We come now to consider other functions performed by banks as commercial institutions of the country, and the authority from which they derive their origin and powers, which have given rise to the second classification named. (Art. 231.) The second arrangement, like the former, is into three classes, namely: (1.) Commercial Banks; (2.) State Banks; and (3.) Private Banks.

COMMERCIAL BANKS.

259. Commercial Banks are banks located in commercial centers, and designed to facilitate commercial intercourse. Their bills are mostly of large denominations, being of $50 to $500, and frequently of $1000 to $10,000. The business of such banks is often conducted by drafts upon each other of such amounts as may suit the convenience of their custom-

QUEST. **256.** When do the holders of bank notes prefer them to specie? — **257.** What advantages do bank notes redeemable in specie on presentation at the bank possess over specie? — **258.** What is the second classification of banks given? — **259.** What are Commercial Banks? What is the size of their bills? What use do commercial banks often make of drafts?

ers. The larger notes and drafts are employed chiefly in adjusting balances between wholesale dealers in commercial centers, as New York and Boston, Philadelphia and Cincinnati, New Orleans and St. Louis; while the smaller notes penetrate the country whose commerce flows naturally to these several centers of trade.

260. The notes of commercial banks appropriately circulate throughout the region of country sustaining commercial relations to the city or commercial center where such banks are located, and either buying thereof or selling thereto. If New York, for example, buys flour of Michigan and Illinois, it affords a reason for the circulation of New York money in these states. But if Georgia and Tennessee sell nothing to Wisconsin, there can be no reason why Wisconsin money should circulate in those states. So, also, if Wisconsin sells nothing to them, there can be no reason why their money should circulate in the latter state.

STATE BANKS.

261. In a general sense all banks that are established by authority of State Legislatures may be regarded as State Banks. But the term as here introduced is employed in a restricted sense. State Banks, then, are banks authorized by the legislatures of the states in which they are situated, and designed more especially to afford a convenient and safe currency for use in the states where they are respectively located. For the purposes of trade within the state in which such banks are situated, their bills, when properly secured and easily converted into specie, are more desirable than the specie, or the bills of foreign commercial banks.

QUEST. **259.** For what are the larger notes and drafts used? — **260.** Where do the notes of commercial banks properly circulate? Illustrate by an example, showing where the money of a state may properly circulate, and where it may not. — **261.** What are State Banks, in a general sense? What are State Banks, in a restricted sense? What is remarked of their bills for purposes of trade within the state in which such banks are situated?

262. The bills of State Banks afford the best possible currency for all ordinary exchanges within the state, when such banks are located at accessible points, and redeem their bills in specie promptly on presentation. They are objectionable only when located at remote and inaccessible points, or when there is inconvenience, uncertainty, or delay in procuring the redemption of their notes in specie.

PRIVATE BANKS.

263. Private Banks are banks established by individuals, and usually under a general provision of law. They afford facilities for the safe-keeping of money, and for conducting exchanges, similar to those of incorporated banks, and like them they receive moneys on notes or drafts payable at their counters, and remit the same, or their drafts therefor, to their correspondents, when notes and drafts have been forwarded to them for collection and transmission of payment.

264. Private Banks, like Commmercial and State Banks, are usually banks of deposit and exchange. They generally, like other banks, discount paper according to their ability and the wants of their customers; but they are not authorized to issue and circulate their own notes as currency, unless they furnish security for the redemption of their issues, as required in the case of other banks. (Art. 255.)

RECAPITULATION.

265. We have seen that men generally are at liberty to select any employments which they may pursue with advantage to themselves and with benefit to the community in which they live; but that no person has a right to do that which works ill to his neighbor, and violates the law of reciprocity.

QUEST. **262.** When are their bills the *best currency*, and when, only, are they objectionable? — **263.** What are Private Banks? How are they useful? — **264.** What other functions do they perform? Do they issue their own notes as currency? — **265.** What employments are men at liberty to select, and what have they no right to do?

266. We have seen that *labor is the source of wealth;* that each man, while obeying the law of reciprocity, has exclusive right to the fruits of his industry; that the wages of the laborer will depend upon his *industry*, his *intelligence*, his *skill*, and his *moral character;* that men should at all events *do something*, and that it is their privilege to devote themselves to the highest and most productive forms of industry for which they have an aptitude, and the necessary skill and trustworthiness, wherever there is a demand for such labor; that each man is under obligation to render to society an equivalent for the benefits he receives, in such form as he may be able; that it is a law of the Creator, *If any man will not work neither shall he eat;* and that the *laborer* and the *capitalist* are mutually interested in each other's well being.

267. We have seen that, in order to render labor most productive, each man engages in producing much of *one*, or at most of a *few things*, while every man's happiness is promoted by the possession and use of a *thousand products;* that each and every one can hence gratify more innocent desires, and enjoy more happiness, by a mutual exchange of surplus products; and that merchants and money contribute to the rapidity, frequency, and cheapness of exchanges, and hence to the general prosperity of the entire community. And beyond this, we have seen how Banks are useful to society for the safe-keeping of money; in the diminution of crime; as offering facilities for exchanges, domestic and foreign, on terms beneficial to every one; how they benefit the borrower and the lender; how they unite and benefit both labor and capital; and how they, in various other ways, advance the welfare of society, and aid in effecting exchanges.

QUEST. **266.** What is said of *labor*, *rights*, and *wages?* Should every man *do something?* To what forms of industry may persons devote themselves? What should every one render to society? What law of the Creator is stated? What of the laborer and the capitalist? — **267.** How is labor rendered most productive, and how is every man's happiness promoted? What of exchanges? What of merchants and money? How are banks useful to society? What is their effect upon borrower and lender? What their effect upon labor and capital?

268. The study and practice of Book-keeping would greatly promote the public good, by facilitating exchanges, and in diminishing the amount of the circulating medium that would otherwise be necessary therefor. The machinery of civil society would be thus more economically carried on, and from the numerous checks that would in this way be thrown about individuals in their public and private intercourse, the temptations to dishonesty would be diminished, and the principles of integrity strengthened.

269. While we have remarked upon the circumstance and conditions that contribute to success in business, and to the welfare of the community at large, the causes of want of prosperity can hardly fail to be manifest. Whenever any of the conditions that have been mentioned as essential to success, are violated or disregarded in any community, then will the prosperity of *individuals* in that community, and of the *whole community*, decline in proportion. There is, and can be, no royal road to riches. Wealth, or a moderate competence even, is generally attainable only as the fruit of long and well-directed industry. Wherever consumption exceeds production, there must abundance and happiness, less or more rapidly, give place to poverty and misery. Men may, for a time, *seem* to be prosperous while violating the law of reciprocity. But *real* prosperity, and *enduring* good, are attainable only by the active employment of our faculties in harmony with the established laws of the Creator.

QUEST. **268.** What would be the effect of the general study and practice of Book-keeping? How would it affect the amount of circulating medium required? What of its "checks" upon individuals?—**269.** When will the prosperity of *individuals*, and of a *community* decline? Is there any royal road to riches? How, only, is wealth, or a competence, attainable? What will result when consumption exceeds production? What is said of *seeming* and *real* prosperity?

PART FOURTH.

DOUBLE ENTRY BOOK-KEEPING.

ART. **270.** DOUBLE ENTRY is a system of Book-keeping in which every transaction is *twice entered;* first on the Dr. side of one or more accounts, and then on the Cr. side of one or more other accounts, to which it also belongs. It is from this circumstance that it derives its name. Double Entry is especially adapted to the wants of persons engaged in a wholesale trade, or in any business which is complicated.

271. In Double Entry Book-keeping three principal books have generally been employed, viz.: a Day Book, a Journal, and a Ledger. But many of our best book-keepers now dispense with the use of one of these books, by combining all that is essential of two, in one, and thereby save to themselves much time and labor in writing. A set of books should contain a distinct and systematic record of all we wish or need to know about our business. That is the best system of Book-keeping which is most easily kept, which enables us most readily and certainly to know the exact state of our affairs, and which is most intelligible to others.

272. In this treatise the Journal and Ledger, only, are used as principal books. The Transactions in the Examples for Practice contain the information usually given in the Day Book. References are made in the Journal, when necessary, showing where sums entered may be found, and on what

---

QUEST. **270.** What is Double Entry Book-keeping? To whose wants is it especially adapted? — **271.** How many principal books are generally kept in double entry, and what are they? With what do many of our best book-keepers dispense? What should a set of books contain? What is the *best system* of Book-keeping? — **272.** In this treatise what books only are used? What references are made in the Journal?

accounts they have been received or paid. These references are generally made either to the Invoice Book, (see entries * **2**, **6**, and **8**, of Journal A,) or to the Sales Book, (see entries **3**, **4**, **5**, etc.) When not to one of these, the nature of the transaction will suggest the proper reference phrase.

DEFINITION OF BOOKS.

273. The INVOICE BOOK is a book in which are entered at length all *Invoices*, or bills of goods *purchased.* It may be made by copying invoices into a blank book, or by pasting the original invoices into a book made for that purpose. When invoices are numbered and placed on file, as recommended in Art. 156, they may be referred to by number.

274. The SALES BOOK is a book in which are entered at length all bills of Mdse. *sold.* (Art. 157.)

275. The JOURNAL either contains the particulars of every business transaction, or it makes special reference to the name and page of the book in which they may be found, or if to papers on file, to their title and number. In it the entries are so recorded that they may be readily posted to their proper accounts in the Ledger. It is ruled like the Day Book in the Third Form of Accounts, but is used differently. The Dr. sums are all entered in the left-hand columns, and the Cr. sums in the right-hand columns.

276. In case there are several Dr. items in an entry, to be posted to as many different accounts, their sum will exactly equal the sum of the Cr. items. In such cases it is customary

* By referring to the entries in the Journal it will be seen that they are numbered in full-faced figures. This has been done in order to facilitate the reference to particular entries in giving explanations of the mode of making the Journal entries, of posting them to their proper accounts in the Ledger, and of balancing the accounts.

QUEST. **272.** To what books are these references generally made? — **273.** What is the Invoice Book? How may it be made? When invoices are numbered and placed on file, how may they be referred to? — **274.** What is the Sales Book? — **275.** What does the Journal contain? How are the entries recorded in it? How is it ruled? Where are the Dr. sums entered, and where the Cr. sums? — **276.** When there are several Dr. items in an entry to be posted to as many different accounts, what will their sum exactly equal?

to use the word "Sundries" before the several particulars that are entered at the Dr. side of the account, as in entries **1** and **6** of Journal A. In entries **2** and **11** the reverse is true, the Dr. entries being posted to one account, and the Cr. entries each to *sundry* accounts. The word "Sundries," however, in such cases, although sometimes employed, is not used in the annexed Journal, nor is it uniformly employed in Dr. entries. The *fact* of there being "Sundries" is apparent, whether the word is employed or not.

277. In all cases the Dr. amount posted from an entry, whether to one or more accounts, should exactly equal the Cr. amount. The general principle is beautifully illustrated in the symbol of a pair of scales on the title-page of the Book-keeping, referred to in Art. 38. The Symbol on the title-page of the Account Books particularly illustrates entry **1**, Journal A. (Page 188.)

278. When a page of the Journal has been written up, the money columns should be footed, and in case the Dr. and Cr. amounts exactly agree, the inference is that the sums have been correctly entered. If they disagree, it is certain a mistake has been made. The work should then be carefully reviewed, and all errors corrected, as directed in Art. 130.

279. Rules for Journalizing. In writing up the Journal, the principles already elucidated for Debtor and Creditor are applicable. (Arts. 16 to 27.) But the usual Dr. and Cr. signs are omitted. The word "To," as employed in the Journal, indicates that the titles of accounts preceding it are Dr., and those following it Cr. Of the many rules for Journalizing that might be given, none, perhaps, are superior

Quest. **276.** What of the word "Sundries" in such cases? When there is one Dr. sum in an entry, and several Cr. items to be posted against it, is the word "Sundries" then used? What *fact* is apparent? — **277.** To what is the Dr. amount posted from an entry in all cases equal? What symbol illustrates the general principle? What symbol particularly illustrates the first entry in the Journal? — **278.** How may you determine whether the Journal entries on a page have been correctly made? When is it certain a mistake has been made? — **279.** What is said of Debtor and Creditor, and the word *To?*

to the following, which may be the better remembered for being expressed in homely verse.

> "By Journal laws what you receive
> Is Debtor made to what you give.
> Stock for your debts must Debtor be,
> And Creditor for property.
> Profit and Loss Accounts are plain;
> You debit Loss and credit Gain."

280. The LEDGER in Double Entry Book-keeping, like that already described, is a book to which the entries recorded in the Journal are transferred and so arranged as to present each account on a folio by itself. The instructions given in relation to the Ledger, and to Posting Books (Arts. 122 to 130) are applicable here. The letter *J*, in the Ledger, stands for Journal.

CLASSES OF ACCOUNTS.

281. The accounts in a merchant's Ledger may be classified under the three following heads, — Real Accounts, Personal Accounts, and Imaginary Accounts.

282. REAL ACCOUNTS include all accounts of effects or things which a person possesses. Of this class are the Cash Account and the Merchandise Account. To these may be added the accounts kept in the First and Second Forms of Account, other than accounts with persons; such as the Cornfield Account, the Beef Account, and the Sheep and Wool Account; also the Stone Mill, and Wagon Shop Accounts in the following Examples for Practice.

283. PERSONAL ACCOUNTS are the accounts kept with different persons with whom we transact business.

284. IMAGINARY ACCOUNTS are fictitious titles invented to represent the person or company that conduct a business,

QUEST. **279.** Give rule for Journalizing. — **280.** What is the Ledger? For what does *J* stand? — **281.** Under how many heads may the accounts in a merchant's Ledger be classified, and what are they? — **282.** What are Real Accounts? Mention some accounts of this class. — **283.** What are Personal Accounts? — **284.** What are Imaginary Accounts?

or to supply the want of some real or personal titles in recording such gains or losses as cannot with propriety be placed to Real or Personal Accounts. Of this class are Stock, Profit and Loss, Expense, and Interest Accounts.

TITLES OF ACCOUNTS.

285. The Stock Account represents the person or company that conduct a business. On the Dr. side of this account are entered all the sums they owe on commencing business, and on the Cr. side, the amount of money and the value of property they carry into business. The excess of the credits over the debits will be the *net* amount of property invested in trade.

286. The Merchandise Account shows how much has been paid for Merchandise, and how much it has been sold for. On the Dr. side of this account are entered the value of all the Merchandise on hand at the time of commencing business, and the amounts paid for all subsequent purchases. On the Cr. side of the account are entered the amounts of all sales. In case the Merchandise is all sold, the difference between the Dr. and the Cr. sides of the account will exhibit the gross gain or loss on Merchandise. If any goods remain unsold, their value should be ascertained by taking an inventory of them, and then be entered on the Cr. side of the account. The mode of doing this and of ascertaining the *gross profit* in trade, and finally the *net gain*, is shown under the head of Balancing Accounts. (Art. 296.)

287. The Expense Account includes all sums that have been paid for carrying on one's business; such as freight, clerk hire, store rent, etc. All such expenses should be en-

Quest. **284.** Mention some accounts of this class. — **285.** What does the Stock Account represent? What sums are entered on the Dr. and what on the Cr. side of this account? How do we arrive at the *net* amount of property invested in trade? — **286.** What does the Merchandise Account show? What entries are made on the Dr. and what on the Cr. side of this account? How is the gain or loss on Merchandise ascertained? — **287.** What does the Expense Account include?

tered on the Dr. side of this account. The Cr. side of this account contains nothing until the closing of the books. The sum necessary to *balance* the account is then entered on the Cr. side, the same amount being likewise entered on the Dr. side of the Profit and Loss Account, as is fully explained under the head of Balancing Accounts. (Art. 296.)

288. The CASH ACCOUNT exhibits the receipts and disbursements of Cash, including specie and bank notes. In it may also be entered certificates of deposit, checks, and drafts, which are the representatives of Cash. (Art. 45.)

289. The PROFIT AND LOSS ACCOUNT, as its title implies, is kept to show the Profits and Losses in one's business. On the Dr. side of this account are entered all *losses* sustained, and all moneys paid for labor, taxes, etc., which do not belong more properly to other accounts, including the sum necessary to balance the Expense Account. On the Cr. side are entered all gains of whatever kind arising from one's business.

290. On closing this account, if the sum of the Cr. entries is *greater* than that of the Dr. entries, the difference will be the amount of Profit that has arisen from the business; but if it is *less*, it will exhibit the amount of Loss sustained.

291. The BALANCE ACCOUNT is the title of an account sometimes employed for the purpose of balancing unclosed accounts; hence its name. In this work the Ledger Balances are obtained without the use of this account.

POSTING BOOKS.

292. The instructions for Posting Books, given in Arts. 127 to 132, are applicable here. Every sum entered in the

QUEST. **287.** On which side of the account are all expenses entered? What does the Cr. side of this account contain? — **288.** What does the Cash Account exhibit? What may be entered in it? — **289.** For what purpose is the Profit and Loss Account kept? What entries are made on the Dr. and what on the Cr. side of this account? — **290.** When does this account represent that a Profit has arisen in business, and when that a Loss has been sustained? — **291.** What is the Balance Account? Is this account opened in the Ledger?

Dr. columns of the Journal is posted into the Ledger to the Dr. side of the account opposite which it stands in the Journal; and every sum entered in the Cr. columns of the Journal is posted to the Cr. side of the account opposite whose title it stands. The reference figures from the page of each book to the page of the other, are entered according to the instructions already referred to. The Journal page is entered in the Ledger at the left of the money columns into which the sum has been posted, and the Ledger page is entered in the Journal opposite the title of the account that has been posted.

293. The *seventeen* Transactions of the following Illustrative Example give rise to the first seventeen Journal entries, numbered **1** to **17** inclusive. When the student is able to journalize these transactions without referring to the Journal for assistance, he may post the entries to the Ledger. Having carefully reviewed his postings to entry **17** inclusive, a Trial Balance should be taken.

TRIAL BALANCE.

294. We have already shown how errors may be detected in Journal entries by adding the sums in the money columns. (Art. 278.) The Trial Balance, which is taken for the purpose of ascertaining whether the Journal entries have been correctly transferred to the Ledger, as well as to prepare the way for balancing unclosed accounts, affords a similar test of the accuracy of postings. Neither test, however, is infallible; for although *right sums* may be entered, and in the *right columns*, still they may be entered to *wrong accounts*. Hence the necessity for constantly exercising great care in writing up all your books.

QUEST. **292.** How are entries posted from the Journal to the Ledger?—**293.** How many Transactions are there in the Illustrative Example, and to how many Journal entries do they give rise? When may the entries be posted to the Ledger? When should the Trial Balance be taken?—**294.** For what purpose is it taken? Why are not the proof tests of adding the money columns of the Journal and the Ledger infallible?

295. The Trial Balance is taken as follows: First, rule a sheet of paper as is done in case of the Trial Balance given at the 204th page. Then the two sides of every account in the Ledger should be added, and the less amount subtracted from the greater. All those accounts which will exactly balance should be ruled off and closed at once. This done, the titles to all our unclosed accounts, and the difference between the footings of the two sides of each account in the Ledger, should be entered in the Trial Balance, on the Dr. side when there is a debit excess in the Ledger account, and on the Cr. side when there is a credit excess. Then, as the sum of all the debit entries posted into the Ledger is exactly equal to the sum of all the credit entries thus posted, and as we have only left off from the Trial Balance those accounts that exactly balance, it is apparent that the sum of all the entries in the Dr. columns of the Trial Balance should exactly agree with the sum of all the entries in the Cr. columns. The sums in these columns should next be added. In case the footings agree, the inference is that the Journal entries have been correctly posted into the Ledger. If they disagree, it is certain a mistake has been made, and the work should be reviewed.

BALANCING ACCOUNTS.

296. Balancing Accounts is a systematic closing of the Ledger Accounts in order to determine whether, on the whole, there has been *gain* or *loss* in trade, how much, and how it has arisen. In the following Illustrative Example the only source of *gain* is from the sale of Merchandise. In case Mdse. has been sold for *more* than it cost and the expenses incurred in carrying on the business, there has been *gain* in trade; but if sold for *less* than its cost and expenses of carrying on the business, there has been *loss.*

QUEST. **295.** Describe at length the mode of taking the Trial Balance. — **296.** What is Balancing Accounts? What is the only source of *gain* in the Illustrative Example? How do we determine whether, on the whole, there has been *gain* or *loss* in trade?

297. Every entry that has appeared in any Ledger Account to the date of the 17th and last transaction recorded, January 30th, has been posted from the Journal. But under date of January 31st there are several Ledger entries, some of which have been posted from the Journal, while others have a different origin. We will see how these have arisen.

298. An Inventory of Mdse. on hand is taken January 31st, when we proceed to balance the unclosed accounts.

The Inventory in the Illustrative Example employed, (Art. 310, p. 187,) shows that

We have on hand Mdse. to the value of . .	$1471.00
We have sold, as per Cr. side of Mdse. Acct.,	9233.60
Total Cr. to Merchandise Account, ...	10704.60
We have paid for Mdse. to Jan. 30th, . . .	9815.00
Balance of Mdse. Acct., *Gross Profits*, . .	$889.60

299. We are now prepared to close the Merchandise Account, which is done as follows: January 31st, we credit Mdse. for the amount on hand as per Inventory. This entry, which is made in the Ledger in Roman letters and figures, and which is frequently entered by the book-keeper in *red ink*, is not brought from the Journal, but is entered as an amount on hand to the credit of Merchandise to be brought down as a Balance. (Arts. 46 and 303.)

300. The Merchandise Account now contains on the Dr. side all we have paid for Merchandise, and on the Cr. side all we have received for Mdse., together with the value of that on hand. The Cr. excess must be our *gross profits* in trade. Having made the calculation in Art. 298, we are prepared to close the Merchandise Account into Profit and Loss,

---

QUEST. **297.** Do any entries except those posted from the Journal appear in the Ledger previous to taking the Trial Balance? — **298.** What is done before proceeding to balance the unclosed accounts of the Ledger? What is Mdse. on hand inventoried at in the present case, and how do we determine the *gross profits* in trade? — **299.** In closing Merchandise Account what entry is made for Mdse. on hand as per Inventory? How is the entry made? — **300.** How is Merchandise Account closed for *gross profits* in trade?

which is done in entry **18** of the Journal. This entry posted, closes the Ledger account with Merchandise, and opens an account with Profit and Loss.

301. All *expenses* that have been incurred in carrying on the business have been posted to the Dr. side of the Expense Account. We are now, therefore, prepared to make Journal entry **19**, which, when posted, closes the Ledger account with Expenses, and places an equal amount to the debit of Profit and Loss.

302. Now, on the Dr. side of Profit and Loss, we have brought all the *expenses* incurred in carrying on the business; and on the Cr. side of this account appear the *gross profits* that have arisen in trade. The excess of the latter over the former it is evident will be the *net gain.* We then make Journal entry **20**, which, when posted, closes the Profit and Loss account, and carries the *net gain* in trade to the credit of Stock. We have thus closed all accounts that affect *gain* or *loss* in trade, into Profit and Loss, which we have closed into Stock.

303. We now proceed to close Merchandise, (for Balance on hand as per Inventory,) Cash, unsettled Personal Accounts, and Stock, into Ledger Balances, of which the Dr. exhibit our Assets, and the Cr. our Net Stock and Liabilities. Balances should be taken from the Ledger at the close of each month, and be brought together in a Book of Balances. The condition and history of each account, and of all the accounts of the Ledger, may then be seen at a glance. The merchant has thus before him a synopsis of his entire business, with its monthly changes and variations, together with a proof of the accuracy of his postings and Ledger Balances.

304. We have thus far shown the order of closing the

QUEST. **301.** How do we close Expense Account? — **302.** What is the condition of Profit and Loss acct. and how do we close it? — **303.** What accounts are closed into Ledger Balances, and what do these balances represent? What is said of a Book of Balances, and what advantages result from its use?

Ledger Accounts, as applied to the following Illustrative Example. The *same principles* are of general application, as is beautifully illustrated in the Diagram on the opposite page. Merchandise and Expenses we have closed into Profit and Loss. (Arts. 300 and 301.) The several departments of Agriculture and branches of Manufactures and Commerce, together with Interest, Discount, Exchange, and all other accounts indicating *gain* or *loss* in business, in like manner close into Profit and Loss. And however numerous these accounts may be, they can all be closed by two Journal entries, as indicated in the following article.

305. Select from the Ledger all accounts that indicate *gain* or *loss* in trade. Take those in which the sum of the Cr. entries exceeds that of the Dr. entries, and make them Dr. in the sums necessary to balance them severally, and pass the amount of the whole to the Cr. of Profit and Loss. Now take the remaining Ledger accounts of this class, in which the sum of the Dr. entries exceeds that of the Cr. entries, and make Profit and Loss Dr. to these accounts in an amount sufficient to balance them severally. Profit and Loss having thus served us by closing all accounts that indicate *gain* or *loss* in trade, we next close *it* into Stock, which is the third and last Journal entry in Balancing.

306. In the Examples for Practice commencing on the 198th page, after journalizing the 60 transactions there given, the 61st Journal entry will be as follows: Sundries Dr., — Merchandise, Interest, Stone Mill, and Wagon Shop, — in amounts to balance them severally, to Profit and Loss. But no particular rules can be given that shall exactly meet every case. The exercise of judgment is therefore necessary.

QUEST. **304.** Are these principles of general application in closing accounts? How many Journal entries will close all accounts indicating *gain* or *loss* in trade into Profit and Loss? Explain the Diagram. — **305.** Explain the mode of making these closing entries. How is Profit and Loss itself closed? — **306.** (The student may consult this paragraph after journalizing the 60 transactions.) What is said of particular rules, and what of the exercise of the judgment in journalizing?

DIAGRAM FOR CLOSING LEDGER.

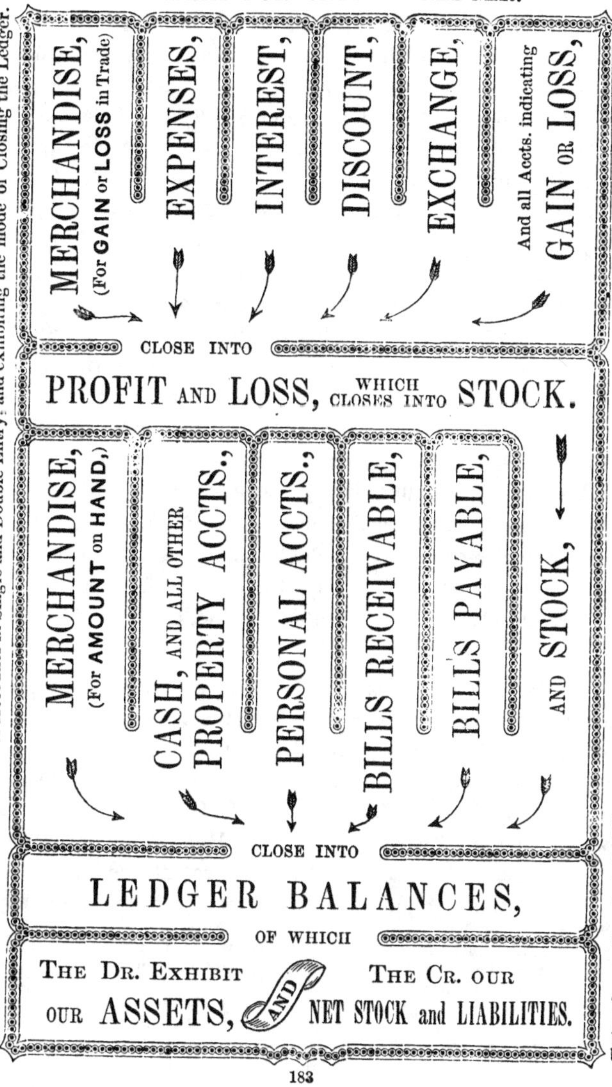

Diagram illustrative of the Relation of Accounts in Single and Double Entry, and exhibiting the mode of Closing the Ledger.

MERCHANDISE, (For GAIN or LOSS in Trade)
EXPENSES,
INTEREST,
DISCOUNT,
EXCHANGE,
And all Accts. indicating GAIN OR LOSS,

CLOSE INTO

PROFIT AND LOSS, WHICH CLOSES INTO STOCK.

MERCHANDISE, (For AMOUNT on HAND,)
CASH, AND ALL OTHER PROPERTY ACCTS.,
PERSONAL ACCTS.,
BILLS RECEIVABLE,
BILLS PAYABLE,
AND STOCK,

CLOSE INTO

LEDGER BALANCES,

OF WHICH

THE DR. EXHIBIT OUR ASSETS, AND THE CR. OUR NET STOCK and LIABILITIES.

307. The form of entry we have observed in closing Expenses, (Art. 301,) will apply to Merchandise, Interest, Stone Mill, or any other account indicating *gain* or *loss* in business, in case the sum of the Dr. entries to it exceeds that of the Cr. entries. And should the Dr. side of Profit and Loss exceed the Cr. side, the difference will go to the Dr. of Stock, and the closing entry of the Journal will be, Stock Dr., for *loss* in trade, to Profit and Loss. The Stock Account will appear among the Dr. Ledger Balances whenever one's Liabilities exceed his Assets, or when he owes more than he possesses. Whatever amount of property one *actually possesses*, above his debts, (if any,) will stand on his Ledger to the Cr. of Stock, and may be considered as a *positive quantity*. But when there is an *actual indebtedness*, beyond one's ability to pay, the amount will stand on his Ledger to the Dr. of Stock, and may be regarded as a *negative quantity*.

308. In the Double Entry Ledger, *J*, as has already been intimated, stands for Journal. The *To* and *By*, which are the usual signs of Dr. and Cr. entries, are often omitted in the Ledger. When a Day Book is used, the Journal entry frequently occupies but a single line, thus:

S. C. Woodward & Co. to Bills Payable.

In such cases two columns are required at the left for post marks: the one at the extreme left for the Dr. entries, and the other for the Cr. entries. In all other respects the Posting should be conducted as from the following Journal to the Ledger. In the above Journal entry, S. C. Woodward & Co., *preceding* the word "to," are Dr., and Bills Payable, *following* it are Cr. (Art. 279.) Dr. sums are entered in the left-hand set of money columns, and Cr. sums in the right-hand set.

QUEST. **307.** To what will the form of entry observed in closing expenses apply? When will Stock be made Dr. in closing Profit and Loss? When will Stock appear among the Dr. Ledger balances? When may Stock be regarded as a *positive* quantity, and when as a *negative* quantity? — **308.** In the Double Entry Ledger what does *J* stand for? What of *To* and *By*? When are two columns required for post-marks? What of posting in other respects? Where are Dr. and Cr. sums entered?

ILLUSTRATIVE EXAMPLE.

FOURTH FORM OF ACCOUNTS.

309. For the purpose of illustrating the method of opening a set of books, and the mode of journalizing and posting transactions, but more especially for the sake of showing clearly and distinctly the method of *closing* a set of books in Double Entry, the following Illustrative Example is here introduced. It can not be too carefully studied.

Monday, January 2d, 1860.

Transaction 1. I commence business this day with the following effects: Merchandise in Store, worth, as per Inventory, $4600.00; Cash in safe, $2500.00; two Notes, one No. 3, against John Otis for $1500.00, and the other, No. 4, against Henry Brown for $1200.00.

Tr. 2. I owe Hill & Wright on account for Mdse. as per Invoice Book A, p. 8, $1350.00, and Clark & Smith, as per Invoice Book A, p. 12, $1250.00.

Tuesday, January 3d, 1860.

Tr. 3. I have this day sold Mdse. to S. C. Wood & Co., as per Sales Book A, p. 15, amounting to $2450.00.

Thursday, January 5th, 1860.

Tr. 4. James Armitage has bought Merchandise of me, on acct., as per Sales Book A, p. 20, amounting to $1240.00.

Friday, January 6th, 1860.

Tr. 5. I have sold Mdse. to several persons, as per Sales Book A, p. 25, amounting to $840.00, for which I have received Cash.

QUEST. 309. Why is the Illustrative Example introduced in Double Entry?

Monday, January 9th, 1860.

Tr 6. I have bought Mdse. in New York, as per Invoice Book A, p. 18, amounting to $2480.00, for which I paid the Cash. My expenses amounted to $30.50, and I paid $65.50 for freight on goods bought.

Tuesday, January 10th, 1860.

Tr. 7. S. C. Wood & Co. have paid me $1650.00 in Cash, on account of Mdse. bought Jan. 3d.

Thursday, January 12th, 1860.

Tr. 8. I have bought Mdse. in Boston, as per Invoice Book A, p. 22, amounting to $1460.00. My expenses amounted to $28.00, and the freight on goods bought was $37.60; all of which I have paid in Cash.

Saturday, January 14th, 1860.

Tr. 9. John Otis has paid his Note, No. 3, of $1,500.00.

Tr. 10. James Armitage has bought Mdse. on acct., as per Sales Book A, p. 30, amounting to $820.00.

Monday, January 16th, 1860.

Tr. 11. I have sold Mdse. for Cash, as per Sales Book A, p. 35, amounting to $1248.60; and Henry Brown has paid his Note, No. 4, of $1200.00.

Wednesday, January 18th, 1860.

Tr. 12. I have paid Hill & Wright $750.00 on acct.; and I have paid Clark & Smith $1250.00 in full of their acct.

Friday, January 20th, 1860.

Tr. 13. S. C. Wood & Co. have bought of me Mdse. on acct., as per Sales Book A, p. 40, amounting to $1850.00.

Monday, January 23d, 1860.

Tr. 14. I have sold Merchandise for Cash, as per Sales Book A, p. 45, amounting to $785.00.

Saturday, January 28th, 1860.

Tr. 15. I have paid Hill & Wright's Draft to M. Drake for $460.00. I have also paid $50.00 for one month's Clerk Hire.

Monday, January 30th, 1860.

Tr. 16. I have bought Mdse. of Hill & Wright, on acct., amounting to $1275.00, as per Invoice Book A, p. 30.

Tr. 17. I have accepted Hill & Wright's Draft in favor of Clark & Smith for $800.00. I have paid $300.00 of this sum in Cash, and the balance is placed to the credit of Clark & Smith in account.

Inventory of Mdse. January 31st, 1860.

310. On taking an Inventory of goods remaining on hand this day, I find I have Merchandise worth $1471.00.

Required to Determine the following Results:

1st. Give the *Trial Balance* taken January 30th, 1860.

2d. Give the *Ledger Balances* as ascertained January 31st, and brought forward under date of February 1st, 1860.

3d. Give the value of my *Assets,* as derived from these Transactions, and state in what they consist.

4th. Give the amount of my *Liabilities,* as derived from these Transactions, and state in what they consist.

5th. Determine the *Net Value of my Stock* Feb. 1, 1860.

6th. Has there been *Gain* or *Loss* in trade during the month of January, and how much?

QUEST. **310.** What is the value of Merchandise on hand, January 31st, as per Inventory? What six results are required?

1 # Journal A.— Double Entry.

			Dr.		Cr.	
		Monday, January 2d, 1860.				
		Sundries Dr.				
1		Merchandise in Store . . .	4600	00		
2		Cash in Safe	2500	00		
3		Bills Receivable				
		No. 3, John Otis, . $1500				
		" 4, Henry Brown, 1200	2700	00		
1	1	To Stock . . .			9800	00
		———— " ————				
1		Stock Dr.				
		Invoice Book A, pp. 8 & 12.	2600	00		
3		To Hill & Wright . .			1350	00
2	2	" Clark & Smith .			1250	00
		———— Jan. 3d. ————				
2		S. C. Wood & Co. Dr.				
		Sales Book A, p. 15 . .	2450	00		
1	3	To Merchandise . .			2450	00
		———— Jan. 5th. ————				
3		James Armitage Dr.				
		Sales Book A, p. 20 . .	1240	00		
1	4	To Merchandise . .			1240	00
		———— Jan. 6th. ————				
2		Cash Dr.				
		Sales Book A, p. 25 . .	840	00		
1	5	To Merchandise . .			840	00
			16930	00	16930	00

Monday, January 9th, 1860. 2

		Dr.		Cr.	
	Sundries Dr.				
1	Merchandise				
	Invoice Book A. p. 18 .	2480	00		
1	Expenses				
	To N. York for Goods, $30.50				
	For Freight on do. 65.50	96	00		
2	**6** To Cash			2576	00
	—— Jan. 10th. ——				
2	Cash Dr.				
	Rec'd of them on Acct. . . .	1650	00		
2	**7** To S. C. Wood & Co.			1650	00
	—— Jan. 12th. ——				
1	Merchandise Dr.				
	Invoice Book A. p. 22 .	1460	00		
1	Expenses				
	To Boston for Goods, $28.00				
	For Freight on do. 37.60	65	60		
2	**8** To Cash			1525	60
	—— Jan. 14th. ——				
2	Cash Dr.				
	Of John Otis, Note No. 3	1500	00		
3	**9** To Bills Receivable .			1500	00
	—— " ——				
3	James Armitage Dr.				
	Sales Book A. p. 30 . . .	820	00		
1	**10** To Merchandise . .			820	00
		8071	60	8071	60

3 *Monday, January 16th, 1860.*

2	Cash Dr.				
	Sales Book A. p. 35 . .	2448	60		
1	To Merchandise . .			1248	60
	Of Henry Brown, Note No. 4				
3	**11** To Bills Receivable .			1200	00
	——— Jan. 18th. ———				
3	Hill & Wright Dr.				
	Paid them on Acct.	750	00		
2	Clark & Smith				
	In full of their Acct. . .	1250	00		
2	**12** To Cash			2000	00
	——— Jan. 20th. ———				
2	S. C. Wood & Co. Dr.				
	Sales Book A. p. 40 . .	1850	00		
1	**13** To Merchandise . .			1850	00
	——— Jan. 23d. ———				
2	Cash Dr.				
	Sales Book A. p. 45 . .	785	00		
1	**14** To Merchandise . .			785	00
	——— Jan. 28th. ———				
3	Hill & Wright Dr.				
	Paid Draft to M. Drake .	460	00		
1	Expenses				
	Clerk Hire 1 mo.	50	00		
2	**15** To Cash			510	00
		7593	60	7593	60

L.F.			Dr.		Cr.	
1	Merchandise Dr.					
	Invoice Book A. p. 30 .		1275	00		
3	16 To Hill & Wright . .				1275	00
	——— " ———					
3	Hill & Wright Dr.					
	For their Draft		800	00		
2	To Clark & Smith .				500	00
2	17 " Cash				300	00
	——— Jan. 31st. ———					
1	Merchandise Dr.					
	Gross Profits in 1 mo. . .		889	60		
3	18 To Profit and Loss .				889	60
	——— " ———					
3	Profit and Loss Dr.					
	Business Expenses 1 mo. .		211	60		
1	19 To Expenses				211	60
	——— " ———					
3	Profit and Loss Dr.					
	Net Gain in 1 mo.		678	00		
1	20 To Stock				678	00
			3854	20	3854	20

NOTE. The last three of the above entries, it should be borne in mind, are not made from Transactions, like the seventeen preceding ones. They arise from the condition of the Ledger. (Arts. 298 to 302.)

INDEX TO LEDGER A.—DOUBLE ENTRY.

A		**H**	
Armitage, James	3	*Hill & Wright*	3
B		**I J K**	
Bills Receivable	3		
C		**L M**	
Cash	2	*Merchandise*	1
Clark & Smith	2		
D		**N O P**	
		Profit and Loss	3
E		**Q R S**	
Expenses	1	*Stock*	1
F		**T U V W**	
		Wood, S. C. & Co.	2
G		**X Y Z**	

Dr. Merchandise Cr.¹

1860.						1860.					
Jan.	2	To J.	1	4600	00	Jan.	3	By J.	1	2450	00
"	9	"	2	2480	00	"	5	"	1	1240	00
"	12	"	2	1460	00	"	6	"	1	840	00
"	30	"	4	1275	00	"	14	"	2	820	00
"	31	"	4	889	60	"	16	"	3	1248	60
						"	20	"	3	1850	00
						"	23	"	3	785	00
						"	31	Invt.		**1471**	**00**
				10704	60					10704	60
Feb.	1	Bal.		1471	00						

Dr. Stock Cr.

1860.						1860.					
Jan.	2	To J.	1	2600	00	Jan.	2	By J.	1	9800	00
"	31	Bal.		7878	00	"	31	"	4	678	00
				10478	00					10478	00
						Feb.	1	Bal.		7878	00

Dr. Expenses Cr.

1860.						1860.					
Jan.	9	To J.	2	96	00	Jan.	31	By J.	4	211	60
"	12	"	2	65	60						
"	28	"	3	50	00						
				211	60					211	60

Dr. Cash Cr.

1860.						1860.					
Jan.	2	To J.	1	2500	00	Jan.	9	By J.	2	2576	00
"	6	"	1	840	00	"	12	"	2	1525	60
"	10	"	2	1650	00	"	18	"	3	2000	00
"	14	"	2	1500	00	"	28	"	3	510	00
"	16	"	3	2448	60	"	30	"	4	300	00
"	23	"	3	785	00	"	31	Bal.		2812	00
				9723	60					9723	60
Feb.	1	Bal.		2812	00						

Dr. Clark & Smith Cr.

1860.						1860.					
Jan.	18	To J.	3	1250	00	Jan.	2	By J.	1	1250	00
"	31	Bal.		500	00	"	30	"	4	500	00
				1750	00					1750	00
						Feb.	1	Bal.		500	00

Dr. S. C. Wood & Co. Cr.

1860.						1860.					
Jan.	3	To J.	1	2450	00	Jan.	10	By J.	2	1650	00
"	20	"	3	1850	00	"	31	Bal.		2650	00
				4300	00					4300	00
Feb.	1	Bal.		2650	00						

Dr. Bills Receivable Cr. 3

Date			F.	Amount		Date			F.	Amount	
1860.						1860.					
Jan.	2	To J.	1	2700	00	Jan.	14	By J.	2	1500	00
						"	16	"	3	1200	00
				2700	00					2700	00

Dr. Profit & Loss Cr.

Date			F.	Amount		Date			F.	Amount	
1860.						1860.					
Jan.	31	To J.	4	211	60	Jan.	31	By J.	4	889	60
"	"		4	678	00						
				889	60					889	60

Dr. Hill & Wright Cr.

Date			F.	Amount		Date			F.	Amount	
1860.						1860.					
Jan.	18	To J.	3	750	00	Jan.	2	By J.	1	1350	00
"	28		3	460	00	"	30	"	4	1275	00
"	30		4	800	00						
"	31	Bal.		615	00						
				2625	00					2625	00
						Feb.	1	Bal.		615	00

Dr. James Armitage Cr.

Date			F.	Amount		Date			F.	Amount	
1860.						1860.					
Jan.	5	To J.	1	1240	00	Jan.	31	Bal.		2060	00
"	14	"	2	820	00						
				2060	00					2060	00
Feb.	1	Bal.		2060	00						

TRIAL BALANCE.

Ans. 1st.

Dr. *January* 30*th*, 1860. *Cr.*

Merchandise, p. 1	*$581*	*40*	*Stock, p. 1*	*$7200*	*00*
Expenses, p. 1	*211*	*60*	*Clark & Smith, p. 2*	*500*	*00*
Cash, p. 2	*2812*	*00*	*Hill & Wright, p. 3*	*615*	*00*
S. C. Wood & Co. 2	*2650*	*00*			
Jas. Armitage, p. 3	*2060*	*00*			
	$8315	*00*		*$8315*	*00*

LEDGER BALANCES.

Ans. 2d.

Dr. *February* 1*st*, 1860. *Cr.*

Merchandise, p. 1	*$1471*	*00*	*Stock, p. 1*	*$7878*	*00*
Cash, p. 2	*2812*	*00*	*Clark & Smith, p. 2*	*500*	*00*
S. C. Wood & Co. 2	*2650*	*00*	*Hill & Wright, p. 3*	*615*	*00*
Jas. Armitage, p. 3	*2060*	*00*			
	$8993	*00*		*$8993*	*00*

Ans. 3d. **MY ASSETS AND THEIR VALUE.**

My Assets, February 1st, 1860, consist of

1st.	Merchandise as per Inventory,	$1471.00	
2d.	Cash, as per Cash Acct., . .	2812.00	
3d.	S. C. Wood & Co. owe me on acct.	2650.00	
4th.	Jas. Armitage owes me on acct.	2060.00	
	Total amount of Assets, ...		$8993.00

	Amount of Assets brought up, . .		$8993.00
Ans. 4th.	MY LIABILITIES, AND TO WHOM.		
1st.	I owe Clark & Smith on acct.	$500.00	
2d.	I owe Hill & Wright on acct.	615.00	
	Total amount of Liabilities, ...		$1115.00
Ans. 5th.	*Net Value of my Stock*, Feb. 1st, 1860,		$7878.00
	Net Value of my Stock, Jan. 2d, 1860,		7200.00
Ans. 6th.	*Net Gain* in trade for January, . .		$678.00

311. The student will find this Illustrative Example solved on pp. 188 to 195, with a full explanation of the whole procedure in Arts. 293 to 303. These may be freely consulted till the learner becomes familiar with the method of *opening, journalizing*, and especially of *closing* a set of books; but he should not pass on till he is so familiar with all the *principles* involved as to be able to explain every step taken without reference to the book. The great beauty of the science of Double Entry is readily apparent in the work of this Example. From the first Journal entry, on page 188, there has been a *perpetual equilibrium* of accounts. The *debits* entered from each transaction have been exactly equal to the *credits*. The footings of the Dr. and Cr. columns of every page of the Journal agree in amount. The equilibrium appears again in the Trial Balance, on the last page, and finally in the Ledger Balances there given. In case the learner acquires a *thorough mastery* of these principles, and is alike thorough with the following but more difficult Examples for Practice, he will readily become an accomplished book-keeper. Is not this result worth the effort?

QUEST. **311.** What is said of the Illustrative Example? What should the learner be able to do before he passes from this example? What is said of the beauty of Double Entry? What of the *equilibrium* of accounts? What will result from a *thorough mastery* of these principles?

EXAMPLES FOR PRACTICE.

FOURTH FORM. — PARTNERSHIP.

312. In PARTNERSHIP each Partner's *individual* dealings with the Firm are conducted in all respects on the same basis as other *personal* accounts. Each is debited for what he receives from the Firm, and for what is paid on his account, and credited for what he brings to the Firm, and for what is received on his account. (See Arts. 199 to 201.)

The Opening Journal Entries of this example will be made on the same principle as were those of the former example; and they will be in amounts as indicated in the Ledger Balances at the 196th page, with this difference: The Cash and Stock will each be $5000.00 more than there, on account of Capital brought to the Firm by the incoming Partner.

Wednesday, February 1st, 1860.

Transaction 1. I have agreed with Phineas Graves to receive him as a Partner in a General Mercantile Business, to be conducted under the title* of "Mayhew & Graves." I put into the business all of my Assets, as given in Ans. 2d of the last example, and the Firm assume my Liabilities, as there given. (See Ledger Balances, p. 196.)

Tr. 2. P. Graves brings with him into the Firm a Cash Capital of $5000.00, and we have agreed to share the *gain* or *loss* in trade equally.

Thursday, February 2d, 1860.

Tr. 3. S. C. Wood & Co. have bought Merchandise of us on account, as per Sales Book B, p. 1, amounting to $140.00.

* Where the author's name is employed in this Example the student may substitute his own name, thus making himself the senior partner of the firm conducting the business. The name adopted must be uniformly employed.

QUEST. **312.** In Partnership how are the partners' *individual* dealings with the Firm conducted? For what is each partner debited, and for what credited? What is remarked of the Opening Journal Entries in Partnership? What partnership has been formed, and with what capital? What is the title of the Firm? Whom will the student regard as the senior partner?

Tr. 4. James Armitage has paid us $1060.00 in Cash, and has given us his Note, No. 1, for $1000.00, payable at our Store in 30 days, with interest at 6 per cent.

Monday, February 6th, 1860.

Tr. 5. We have bought a Wagon Shop, and lot, of Henry L. Haywood, for $900.00, with tools and stock inventoried at $400.00. We give him in payment $500.00 in Cash, and our Note, No. 1, for the balance, at 30 days without interest.

We propose to keep an acct. with *Wagon Shop*. (Arts. 39 and 40.)

Tuesday, February 7th, 1860.

Tr. 6. We have bought Mdse. of S. C. Hooker & Co. of New York, as per Invoice No. 1, amounting to $2750.00. Our expenses attending the purchase were $37.40, and we paid freight on goods, $45.10. We gave our Note, No. 2, to Hooker & Co., for $2250.00, payable at the Exchange Bank in 3 months, with interest at 6 per cent. after 30 days. The balance of Invoice and our expenses we paid in Cash.

Saturday, February 11th, 1860.

Tr. 7. John Porter has bought a bill of Mdse. of us, as per Sales Book B, p. 8, amounting to $1186.00. Of this sum he has paid $326.00 in Cash, and the balance we charge him in account.

Monday, February 13th, 1860.

Tr. 8. We have purchased a stock of Lumber of Henry King, for Wagon Shop, to the amount of $1775.60. We have paid him $225.60 in Cash. The balance of the purchase is on account.

Wednesday, February 15th, 1860.

Tr. 9. We have leased of John Johnson a Stone Flouring Mill, worth $12000.00, for five years. The rent agreed upon is 10 per cent. per annum of the value of the property at this time. We pay 3 months' rent in advance; we also pay $256.00 in Cash for sundry fixtures received with the Mill.

We propose to keep an account with *Stone Mill.* (Arts. 39 and 40.)

Thursday, February 16th, 1860.

Tr. 10. We have sold Mdse. to Isaac Newton, on acct., as per Sales Book B, p. 16, amounting to $280.50.

Monday, February 20th, 1860.

Tr. 11. We have bought of James Bronson 1860 bushels of White Wheat for Stone Mill, at $1.20 a bushel, for which we have given our Note, No. 3, payable in 10 days, in Wagons and Sleighs.

Wednesday, February 22d, 1860.

Tr. 12. We have sold to John Porter 8 Cutters, at $45.00 each, and 1 Buggy for $120.00, and charged the same to him in account.

Friday, February 24th, 1860.

Tr. 13. Ira Mayhew has taken from the Wagon Shop a Cutter, for his own use, worth $45.00, and Phineas Graves has taken a Sleigh, worth $50.00, which are charged to them in account.

Monday, February 27th, 1860.

Tr. 14. We have bought $2800.00 worth of Mdse. of Henry Underwood, as per Invoice No. 2, for which we have delivered to him, at the Stone Mill, 300 bbls. of Flour, at $6.00 a barrel. We have paid him the balance of Invoice out of the Wagon Shop, in Buggies, at $125.00 each.

Wednesday, February 29th, 1860.

Tr. 15. We have purchased of Henry Hathaway 901 and $\frac{1}{49}$ bush. of Red Wheat at 98 c. a bush. and 650 bushels of White Wheat at $1.02 a bushel, for use in the Stone Mill, and have paid him for the same in Mdse.

Thursday, March 1st, 1860.

Tr. 16. Joseph White, who has purchased of James Bronson our Note, No. 3, given Feb. 20th, has presented the same for payment. He takes 20 Lumber Wagons at $75.00 each, and the balance of the Note in Double Sleighs at $61.00 each.

Friday, March 2d, 1860.

Tr. 17. James Armitage has paid his Note, No. 1, given Feb. 2d, with interest. (See transaction of that date.)

We now open an acct. with Interest. (See Arts. 39 and 40.)

Tuesday, March 6th, 1860.

Tr. 18. We have paid our Note, No. 1, given to H. L. Haywood Feb. 6th. He took on it 130 bbls. of Flour at $6.00 a barrel, and the balance of the Note he received in Shorts from the Stone Mill at $10.00 a ton.

Wednesday, March 7th, 1860.

Tr. 19. John Hinman has bought of us, on acct., 200 bbls. of Flour at $6.00 a barrel, and 8 Lumber Wagons at $65.00 each.

Friday, March 9th, 1860.

Tr. 20. We have sold to Clark & Smith, on acct., 12 Carriages at $75.00 each; 85 bbls. of Flour at $6.00 a barrel; and 20 tons of Ship Stuff at $15.00 a ton.

Saturday, March 10th, 1860.

Tr. 21. We have bought 2700 bushels of Wheat at $1.00 a bushel, and 1900 bbls. at 31 c. each, to be delivered at the Stone Mill. We have paid the foreman in the Wagon Shop $50.00 for 1 month's services. We have also paid $1270.00 for stock, as per Invoice No. 3, for Wagon Shop, all of which has been paid in Cash.

Monday, March 12th, 1860.

Tr. 22. Hill & Wright have bought of us, on acct., 250 bbls. of Flour at $6.00 a barrel, and 5 Lumber Wagons at $65.00 each.

Wednesday, March 14th, 1860.

Tr. 23. We have sold Merchandise to John Paywell, as per Sales Book B, p. 40, amounting to $2400.00. He has also purchased of us 3 Lumber Wagons at $65.00 each, for all of which he has given us his indorsed Note, No. 2, payable at the Exchange Bank in 30 days, with interest at 7 per cent.

Friday, March 16th, 1860.

Tr. 24. We have sold Isaac Newton, on acct., one Lumber Wagon for $60.00; 20 bbls. of Superfine Flour at $6.50 each; and 10 bbls. of Flour at $6.00 a barrel.

Monday, March 19th, 1860.

Tr. 25. We have bought of Isaac Newton, on acct., an assorted stock of Wood for Wagon Shop, for $265.00. We have also bought of Hill & Wright, on acct., a bill of Hardware for Wagon Shop, as per Invoice No. 4, amounting to $387.50.

Tuesday, March 20th, 1860.

Tr. 26. We have bought Merchandise in New York, as per Invoice No. 5, amounting to $2944.00. Our expenses to New York were $24.00, and we paid $27.00 for freight on goods bought, for all of which we have paid Cash.

Thursday, March 22d, 1860.

Tr. 27. H. King has presented the Order of Ira Mayhew at the Wagon Shop, on which he has received one Lumber Wagon worth $65.00.

Tr. 28. We have this day paid Store Expenses in Cash, as follows: for Clerk Hire $75.00, and for Fuel and Lights $30.00.

Saturday, March 24th, 1860.

Tr. 29. Two Orders drawn by Phineas Graves for persons in his private employ, have been presented and paid; one for Flour and Shorts at the Stone Mill for $65.00; and the other for $70.60 in Mdse.

Monday, March 26th, 1860.

Tr. 30. We have sold to Simeon Rice 560 bbls. of Flour from the Stone Mill, at $6.00 a barrel, and received his indorsed Note, No. 3, therefor, payable in 60 days at the Exchange Bank, with interest at 7 per cent.

Tr. 31. We have sold $225.00 worth of Mdse. to John Porter, on acct., as per Sales Book B, p. 60, and 25 bbls. of Flour at $6.00 a barrel.

Tuesday, March 27th, 1860.

Tr. 32. We have bought, on acct., an assorted stock of Wood, of Henry King, for use at the Wagon Shop, worth $230.00. John Porter has completed the wood work of 8 Buggies at $19.00 each, and Isaac Newton has finished the wood work of 10 Sleighs at $17.00 each, for which we credit them in acct.

Thursday, March 29th, 1860.

Tr. 33. S. C. Wood & Co. have given us their Note, No. 4, to balance their acct. Said Note is payable at the Exchange Bank the 1st of May, and draws interest from February 1st at 6 per cent. per annum.

Friday, March 30th, 1860.

Tr. 34. We have given to James Armitage an Order on the Stone Mill for 25 bbls. of Flour worth $6.00 a barrel, and 2 tons of Shorts worth $10.00 a ton, and charged the same to him in account.

313. The learner having written up his Journal to this date, and posted the same to the Ledger, should take a *Trial Balance* before proceeding further. (Art. 294.) In case he obtains the following result he may conclude his work is correct, and proceed in journalizing; otherwise the work of the Journal and Ledger should be reviewed and corrected.

Dr. TRIAL BALANCE, MARCH 30TH, 1860. *Cr.*

Merchandise, p. 1	4116	90	Stock, p. 3	12878	00
Cash, p. 2	629	90	Interest, p. 6	5	00
Jas. Armitage, p. 4	170	00	Bills Payable, p. 7	2250	00
John Hinman, p. 4	1720	00	Henry King, p. 7	1780	00
Clark & Smith, p. 5	1210	00	Stone Mill, p. 11	2422	00
Phin. Graves, p. 5	185	60	Wagon Shop, p. 12	271	90
Hill & Wright, p. 6	822	50			
Bills Receivable, 8	8745	00			
Ira Mayhew, p. 8	110	00			
Isaac Newton, p. 9	95	50			
Expenses, p. 10	238	50			
John Porter, p. 10	1563	00			
	19606	90		19606	90

314. The page is given, in the preceding Trial Balance, to conform to the page of the Ledger as the example is worked in the Key. The balances to these several accounts will be the same, regardless of the Ledger pages they occupy. The learner, I need hardly here add, has a right to feel encouraged with his progress in proportion as he is able to obtain correct results without aid from his teacher, and without consulting the Key.

QUEST. **313.** What is said in relation to taking a Trial Balance? — **314.** Will the result of the Trial Balance depend in any degree upon the arrangement of accounts in the Ledger?

Tuesday, April 3d, 1860.

Tr. 35. S. C. Wood & Co. have received from Henry King his Draft on us for $1275.00, which we accept. We pay them $125.00 in Cash, furnish them with a Carriage from the Wagon Shop worth $225.00, and place the balance of the Draft to their credit in acct.

Thursday, April 5th, 1860.

Tr. 36. Clark & Smith present an Order on us from Henry King for $125.00, which we accept. They deliver at the Stone Mill on acct., 325 bushels of Wheat worth 95 c. a bushel. We settle our acct. and they give us their Note, No. 5, for balance of acct., payable at our Store in 30 days without interest.

Friday, April 6th, 1860.

Tr. 37. We sell $2500.00 worth of Merchandise to James Armitage, on acct., as per Sales Book B, p. 75.

Monday, April 9th, 1860.

Tr. 38. We sell to John Hinman, on acct., 8 Lumber Wagons at $65.00 each; 160 bbls. of Flour at $6.00 a barrel; and $327.75 worth of Mdse., as per Sales Book D, p. 1.

Thursday, April 12th, 1860.

Tr. 39. We have bought Barns & King's Note, No. 6, of John Hinman for $3000.00. Said Note is indorsed by Hinman to us, has drawn interest from February 1st at 6 per cent., and is payable May 21st at the Exchange Bank. We credit Hinman in acct. for the Note, and allow him interest on same for 2 months and 10 days. Hinman this day furnishes us with Invoice, No. 6, of Lumber for Wagon Shop, amounting to $254.60.

Saturday, April 14th, 1860.

Tr. 40. John Paywell has this day taken up his Note,

No. 2, given the 14th of March, payable at the Exchange Bank,* and drawing interest.

Monday, April 16th, 1860.

Tr. 41. We have bought Mdse. in Boston of Josiah Wall, as per Invoice No. 6, amounting to $3400.00. Our expenses attending the purchase were $35.00, and we have paid $23.00 freight on goods bought. We have given our Note, No. 4, for $2500.00, payable in 60 days. Our expenses and the balance of Invoice were paid in Cash.

Friday, April 20th, 1860.

Tr. 42. We have sold S. C. Wood & Co. Mdse., on acct., as per Sales Book D, p. 10, amounting to $1125.50; 8 Buggies at $105.00 each; and 60 bbls. of Flour at $6.00 a bbl.

Monday, April 23d, 1860.

Tr. 43. James Armitage buys of us one Single Wagon for $125.00, and 20 bbls. of Superfine Flour at $6.50 a barrel. He pays us a Certificate of Deposit of $2500.00 with the Exchange Bank, where we keep our bank account, and which we use as money. The overplus we pass to his credit in acct.

Thursday, April 26th, 1860.

Tr. 44. S. C. Wood & Co. have paid us $500.00 in Cash, on acct., and have delivered at the Stone Mill for us 800 bushels of Wheat at $1.05 a bushel.

Tuesday, May 1st, 1860.

Tr. 45. S. C. Wood & Co. have paid their Note, No. 4, of March 29th, due this day at the Exchange Bank with interest.

* We keep our Bank Acct. with the Exchange Bank, and any moneys paid us there we place to the debit of Cash. Notes of ours falling due at the bank, and paid by the bank for us, we place to the credit of Cash, as though paid by us in person.

Thursday, May 3d, 1860.

Tr. 46. James Armitage has bought Merchandise of us, on acct., as per Sales Book D, p. 25, amounting to $1240.75.

Tr. 47. John Hinman has bought of us, on acct., as follows: Mdse. as per Sales Book D, p. 30, amounting to $1422.00, and 20 bbls. of Flour at $6.40 a barrel.

Saturday, May 5th, 1860.

Tr. 48. Clark & Smith have paid us their Note, No. 5, given April 5th.

Monday, May 7th, 1860.

Tr. 49. We have paid our Note, No. 2, given to S. C. Hooker & Co. Feb. 7th, and this day due at the Exchange Bank.

Tuesday, May 8th, 1860.

Tr. 50. Henry King has delivered $475.00 worth of Lumber at the Wagon Shop on our account, as per Invoice No. 7. He presents an Order on us from Phineas Graves for $125.00, $75.00 of which we pay in Cash, and place the balance to the credit of King in acct.

Thursday, May 10th, 1860.

Tr. 51. Isaac Newton delivers for us at the Stone Mill 603 bushels of Wheat at $1.00 a bushel, and brings an Order on us from Ira Mayhew for $240.00, on which he receives $124.50 in Cash. He buys of us 24 Lumber Wagons at $60.00 each; all of which is entered in account.

Saturday, May 12th, 1860.

Tr. 52. S. C. Wood & Co. have made an assignment, and offer to their creditors 60 cents on a dollar. We settle with them on this basis, and take an accepted Order on James Armitage for the amount agreed upon, which we charge to Armitage in acct.

Tuesday, May 15th, 1860.

Tr. 53. We pay 3 months' Rent of Stone Mill at the rate named in the transaction of February 15th.

Friday, May 18th, 1860.

Tr. 54. We have sold Hill & Wright Mdse., on acct., as per Sales Book D, p. 36, to the amount of $750.00, and 25 bbls. of Flour from the Stone Mill at $6.00 a barrel.

Monday, May 21st, 1860.

Tr. 55. Barns & King have paid their Note, No. 6, which we received of John Hinman April 12th. (For amount, time, etc., see transaction of that date.)

Wednesday, May 23d, 1860.

Tr. 56. We have sold our interest in the Lease of the Stone Mill, taken February 15th, with the fixtures then purchased, and stock in Mill, to T. Hill for $1680.00, Cash. Hill has also bought of us one Carriage for $185.00, and one Cutter for $40.00.

Saturday, May 26th, 1860.

Tr. 57. Simeon Rice has paid his Note, No. 3, given March 26th, with interest, as per transaction of that date.

Monday, May 28th, 1860.

Tr. 58. We have settled with hands employed in Wagon Shop, and paid $1062.30 in Cash for Labor and Stock to date. We have also paid $2203.25 for Labor and Stock for Stone Mill to date. These sums are in addition to amounts heretofore paid for these purposes.

Tuesday, May 29th, 1860.

Tr. 59. We have bought Merchandise as per Invoice No. 8, amounting to $2212.00. Our expenses attending the purchase, including freight and insurance, were $32.62. We gave in payment our Note, No. 5, to Hatch & Jones, of New York, for $1200.00, payable at the Exchange Bank in 30 days. The balance of invoice and expenses we paid in Cash.

Wednesday, May 30th, 1860.

Tr. 60. We have attended the Mechanics' Fair, and exhibited samples of Merchandise, of Wagons, and of Flour. We receive a Cash premium of $30.00 on Wagons, and another of $20.00 on Flour. Our expenses in attending the Fair have been $45.50. (Profit and Loss.)

Inventory of our Effects, May 31st, 1860.

315. On taking an Inventory of goods we find we have on hand Merchandise in Store worth $3587.52.

On taking an Inventory of Wagon Shop, and Stock in Shop, we find they are together worth $900.00.

Required to Determine the following Results:

1st. Give the *Trial Balance* taken May 30th, 1860.

2d. Give the *Ledger Balances* as ascertained May 31st, and brought forward under date of June 1st, 1860.

3d. Give the Value of our *Assets,* as derived from these Transactions, and state in what they consist.

4th. Give the Amount of our *Liabilities,* as derived from these Transactions, and state in what they consist.

5th. Determine the *Net Value of our Stock,* June 1, 1860.

6th. Give the *Net Value of Stock* belonging to *each Partner,* after paying his indebtedness to the Firm. (Art. 312, Trs. 1 and 2, p. 198.)

These several results, which it is required to determine, and the calculation for the 6th and last, are given on the two following pages. On obtaining them, the learner has occasion for congratulation.

TRIAL BALANCE.

Ans. 1st.

Dr. *May* 30*th*, 1860. *Cr*

Merchandise	2362	90	Stock	12878	00
Cash	10046	67	Interest	98	69
Jas. Armitage	1702	05	Bills Payable	3700	00
John Hinman	1788	15	Henry King	905	00
Phineas Graves	310	60	Profit & Loss	25	80
Hill & Wright	1722	50	Stone Mill	1575	00
Ira Mayhew	350	00	Wagon Shop	1855	00
Isaac Newton	817	00			
Expenses	374	62			
John Porter	1563	00			
	21037	49		21037	49

LEDGER BALANCES.

Ans. 2d.

Dr. *June* 1*st*, 1860. *Cr.*

Merchandise	3587	52	Stock	18182	49
Cash	10046	67	Bills Payable	3700	00
Jas. Armitage	1702	05	Henry King	905	00
John Hinman	1788	15			
Phineas Graves	310	60			
Hill & Wright	1722	50			
Ira Mayhew	350	00			
Isaac Newton	817	00			
John Porter	1563	00			
Wagon Shop	900	00			
	22787	49		22787	49

Ans. 3d. The Dr. Ledger Balances on the opposite page are our *Assets*, and consist of Merchandise, Cash, Wagon Shop, and Personal Accounts, amounting to $22787.49.

Ans. 4th. The Cr. Ledger Balances, except Stock, are our *Liabilities*, and consist of Bills Payable, and a Personal Account we owe Henry King, amounting to $4605.00.

Ans. 5th. The *Net Value of our Stock*, including the indebtedness of both Partners to the Firm, is $18182.49.

Ans. 6th. Net Value of Ira Mayhew's Stock after paying his personal indebtedness to the Firm, $10180.245.

Net Value of Phineas Graves's Stock after paying his personal indebtedness to the Firm, $7341.645.

Although the calculation for determining the Net Stock of each Partner is given below, still the learner will derive advantage from making his own analysis, and reaching the result himself, as he will be compelled to do in actual business.

Calculation for Ira Mayhew's Net Stock.

Net value of our Stock June 1st, ...	$18182.49
Net value of our Stock Feb. 1st, ...	12878.00
Net Gain to be divided equally, ...	$5304.49
Net Gain of each Partner, ...	$2652.245
Ira Mayhew's Stock February 1st, ...	7878.00
Ira Mayhew's Assets June 1st, ...	$10530.245
Deduct his indebtedness to Firm, ...	350.00
Ira Mayhew's *Net Stock*, ...	$10180.245

Calculation for Phineas Graves's Net Stock.

Stock of Phineas Graves Feb. 1st, ...	$5000.00
Net Gain of each Partner, ...	2652.245
Phineas Graves's Assets June 1st, ...	$7652.245
Deduct his indebtedness to Firm, ...	310.60
Phineas Graves's *Net Stock*, ...	$7341.645

Notes and Bills

No.	Date.		Maker's Name.	Indorser's Name.
	1860.			
No. 1	Feb.	2	James Armitage	None
" 2	Mar.	14	John Paywell	Henry Howard
" 3	"	26	Simeon Rice	John Osgood
" 4	"	29	S. C. Wood & Co.	None
" 5	Apr.	5	Clark & Smith	None
" 6	Feb.	1	Barns & King	John Hinman

Notes and Bills

No.	Date.		Payee's Name.	Indorser's Name.
	1860.			
No. 1	Feb.	6	H. L. Haywood	None
" 2	"	7	S. C. Hooker & Co.	James Bronson
" 3	"	20	James Bronson	None
" 4	Apr.	16	Josiah Wall	James Bronson
" 5	May	29	Hatch & Jones	James Bronson

The above is the Bill Book employed in the solution of the Examples for Practice commencing on the 198th page. The most of the Notes here entered, were given, or received, at the time of their date. But this is not the case with Bill Receivable No. 6, as will appear by referring to the transaction of April 12th, page 205. Still, this entry is correct.

Receivable.

When due.		Where Payable.	Amount.		Remarks.
1860.					
Mar.	2	Our Store	$1000	00	Paid at Maturity
Apr.	14	Exchange Bank	2595	00	Paid at Maturity
May	26	Exchange Bank	3360	00	Paid at Maturity
"	1	Exchange Bank	2790	00	Paid at Maturity
"	5	Our Store	776	25	Paid at Maturity
"	21	Exchange Bank	3000	00	Paid at Maturity

Payable.

When due.		Where Payable.	Amount.		Remarks.
1860.					
Mar.	6	Our Store	$800	00	Paid at Stone Mill
May	7	Exchange Bank	2250	00	Paid at Maturity
Mar.	1	Wagon Shop	2232	00	Paid to J. White
June	16	Our Store	2500	00	
"	29	Exchange Bank	1200	00	

These entries were all made at the time the Notes were severally given, or received, except those under the head of "Remarks." Bills Payable, Nos. 4 and 5, not having become due, June 1st, are not entered as paid. (Art. 315.) The statement here made agrees with those of the Trial Balance and Ledger Balances on the preceding folio, as it should.

ILLUSTRATIVE EXAMPLE.

FIFTH FORM OF ACCOUNTS.

316. The science of Double Entry, when thoroughly understood, may be employed in a variety of Forms, having reference to the nature of the business in which one is engaged. The Fourth Form, which may be used in almost any kind of business, is particularly adapted to diversified trading operations, as applied in the last Example for Practice. (Pages 198 to 211.)

317. The Fifth Form is well adapted to a *retail* mercantile business in which the purchases are few in number, but of large amount, while the *sales* are numerous, but being in small amounts it is desirable to bring those of a week or a month together before posting. To meet this necessity, an extra set of money columns is employed for Crs. to Mdse., into which *sales* are carried. But the entries in the one Dr. column, it will be seen, are equal to those in the two Cr. columns taken together. While this arrangement requires but little more writing than when books are kept by *single entry*, it still exhibits more complete and satisfactory results. The example in the Fifth Form, given on pp. 216 to 218, combines with the simplicity of Single Entry, the completeness of results for which Double Entry is so distinguished.

318. Cash sales may be entered in the Journal from the Cash Book once a week, or the receipts of the Money Drawer for the Cash sales of the day may be entered in the Journal every evening, and the amount of such sales may be posted to the Ledger at the end of the month. The Ledger being the same as in other Forms of account it is not necessary here to represent it.

QUEST. **316.** May different forms be employed when books are kept by double entry? To what is the Fourth Form adapted? — **317.** To what is the Fifth Form adapted? Explain its use. What is said of the *labor* and *results* of this method as compared with *single entry*? — **318.** What is said of entering and posting cash sales?

319. Where *purchases* are small and frequent an additional Mdse. Dr. column may be employed, as in case of *sales.* This Form is applicable to the wants of Teachers, Professional Men, and Mechanics, as well as to Merchants. All that is necessary in such cases is to say, *Tuition* Cr., *Services* Cr., or *Shop* Cr., as the case may be, instead of saying, as in this case, Mdse. Cr.

320. When the learner has carefully studied the following Illustrative Example, he will do well to write out a statement of Assets and Liabilities at the time of opening the Journal, under its proper date, together with a statement of the Transactions entered in the Example, under their respective dates. This done, the Illustrative Example here written up may be laid aside, and the pupil may reproduce the Journal from his own statement of Assets, Liabilities, and Transactions. Such exercises will give him a readiness in journalizing which it is difficult otherwise to attain. Beyond this, it will be advantageous for him to post his own Journal, obtain a Trial Balance, make the necessary Closing Journal Entries, post these, and then determine and enter the final Ledger Balances, there being $2160.00 worth of Mdse. on hand, as per Inventory. These exercises may be worked on a few separate sheets ruled by the pupil. The results should agree with those on the 218th page. In posting the Journals of the Fifth and Sixth Forms, the separate Crs. to Mdse. may be checked (thus $\sqrt{}$) to avoid mistakes, they being together posted to the Cr. of Mdse. at the end of the month. This arrangement, it will be seen, requires the posting of but one entry a month, to the Cr. of Mdse., and still, although there may be fifty sales a day, the amount of these sales is carried along, from day to day, in the Journal, till the aggregate sales of the month are posted to the Ledger.

QUEST. **319.** When may a Mdse. Dr. column be employed? — To whose wants beside Merchants is this form applicable, and how? — **320.** What statement is the learner advised to prepare concerning the Illustrative Example in this Form?

1 *Boston, Tuesday, May 1st, 1860.*

L. F.		Sund's	Dr.	Sund's	Cr.	Mdse.	Cr.
2	Sundries To Stock . . .			3800	00		
1	Merchandise in Store .	2700	00				
1	Cash in Safe and Bank	475	00				
2	Bills Rec. No.1,J.Brooks,B.B.	275	00				
2	John Cook Bal. of his acct.	350	00				
	——— " ———						
2	Stock To Sundries . . .	450	00				
3	" John Hill on acct.			230	00		
4	" Bills Pay. No.1 ,B.B.			220	00		
	——— *May 4th.* ———						
3	John Hill To Mdse. . .					48	30
	20 lbs. Sugar @ 9 c. . .	1	80				
	9 Yds. Bl'k Cloth @ $4.50	40	50				
	2 Boxes Raisins @ $3.00	6	00				
	——— *May 5th.* ———						
1	Cash Sales this week per C.B.	125	00				
√	To Mdse. . . .					125	00
	——— *May 8th.* ———						
3	Wm. Cook To Mdse. . .					15	88
	14 lbs. Putty @ 8 c. . .	1	12				
	12 Yds. Bl'k Silk @ 90 c.	10	80				
	44 " Cotton Cloth @ 9 c.	3	96				
	——— *May 10th.* ———						
3	Store Expenses						
	For Rep'rs on Store per Bill	15	50				
3	To H. Allen . .			15	50		
	——— *May 12th.* ———						
1	Cash Sales this week per C. B.	200	00				
√	To Mdse. . . .					200	00
	——— *May 14th.* ———						
3	John Hill						
	For Order to his Son	24	35				
√	To Mdse. . . .					24	35
	Mdse. carried forward			413	53	413	53
		4679	03	4679	03		

L. F.		Sund's Dr.		Sund's Cr.		Mdse. Cr.	
	Mdse. brought forward	413	53			413	53
2	John Cook To Mdse. . .					17	12
	26 Yds. Sheeting @ 25 c.	6	50				
	12 " Blue Silk @ 75 c.	9	00				
	18 lbs. Cru'd Sugar @ 9c.	1	62				
	May 19th.						
4	Family Expenses						
	Sund's for use at the house	32	15				
√	To Mdse. . . .					22	15
1	" Cash . . .			10	00		
	"						
1	Cash Sales this week per C.B.	227	60				
√	To Mdse. . . .					227	60
	May 21st.						
3	Wm. Cook For his Order	52	00				
4	To Ira Graves .			20	00		
√	" Mdse. . . .					32	00
	May 26th.						
1	Cash Sales this week per C.B.	225	50				
√	To Mdse. . . .					225	50
	May 28th.						
4	Ira Graves To Mdse. . .					10	90
	10 lbs. Cru'd Sugar @ 9 c.		90				
	4 Yds. Cassimere @ $2.50	10	00				
	May 30th.						
3	Store Expenses						
	For 1 Chandelier. .	8	00				
1	To Cash . . .			8	00		
	May 31st.						
4	Ira Graves To Mdse. . .					3	82
	8 Yds. Cambric @ 9 c. .		72				
	10 " Gingham @ 31 c.	3	10				
1	Total Mdse. Credits for month			952	62	952	62
		990	62	990	62		

When the learner has posted the Illustrative Example journalized on pp. 216 and 217, and has observed the directions in Art. 320, (page 215,) he will be prepared to answer the following questions:

1st. What is the Trial Balance from this Journal?

2d. What are the final Ledger Balances?

3d. What has been the Net Gain in business?

TRIAL BALANCE.

Ans. 1st.

Dr. *May* 31*st*, 1860. *Cr.*

Merchandise, p. 1	1747	38	Stock, p. 2	3350	00
Cash, p. 1	1235	10	John Hill, p. 3	157	35
Bills Receivable, 2	275	00	Henry Allen, p. 3	15	50
John Cook, p. 2	367	12	Ira Graves, p. 4	5	28
William Cook, p. 3	67	88	Bills Payable, p. 4	220	00
Store Expenses, p. 3	23	50			
Family Expen. p. 4	32	15			
	3748	13		3748	13

LEDGER BALANCES.

Ans. 2d.

Dr. *June* 1*st*, 1860. *Cr.*

Merchandise, p. 1	2160	00	Stock, p. 2	3706	97
Cash, p. 1	1235	10	John Hill, p. 3	157	35
Bills Receivable, 2	275	00	Henry Allen, p. 3	15	50
John Cook, p. 2	367	12	Bills Payable, p. 4	220	00
William Cook, p. 3	67	88	Ira Graves, p. 4	5	28
	4105	10		4105	10

Ans. 3d. Net Gain in business, $356.97.

ILLUSTRATIVE EXAMPLE.

SIXTH FORM OF ACCOUNTS.

321. In the Sixth Form the Journal contains separate Dr. and Cr. columns for Cash, which enables us to combine the Cash Book with the Journal. This Form is especially adapted to a business in which there are many Cash transactions, as in Banking and Exchange, where moneys are frequently received from depositors, and often paid to them, or on their checks. All Cash received or paid is entered in the *Cash* columns, and all other transactions are carried to the columns for *Sundries*. The titles of accounts requiring Dr. entries are written first, with the amounts belonging to them entered opposite, at the left hand, in the Dr. columns. The Cr. titles are then written, after the word "To," with the amounts belonging to them entered at the right hand, in the Cr. columns. (Arts. 279 and 308.)

322. At the close of each day a *Cash Balance* is entered. In the annexed Journal the *footings* of the Cash columns, and the *Balance*, are entered at the close of the day in *italics;* (but by the book-keeper usually in *red ink.*) The Cash Balance at the close of the first day (June 2d) is obtained by taking the sum of the Cash credits from the sum of the debits to Cash. After the first day Cash Balances are uniformly obtained by adding the Cash receipts of the day to the *Balance* of the previous day, and subtracting from this sum the amount of Cash paid out during the day. In obtaining the Balance for June 4th, it should be observed that the two Dr. entries to Cash, on page 1 of the following Journal, must be added with the Dr. entries, on page 2, the account for that day having been commenced on one page and continued on the other. The Balances thus obtained should at all times exactly equal in amount the Cash on hand.

QUEST. **321.** What does the Journal contain in the Sixth Form? How are entries made in the Journal? — **322.** When and how are *cash balances* obtained?

323. At the foot of each page of the Journal a *Proof* is obtained by bringing the Dr. and Cr. Cash footings under those of Sundries, and adding them together. In case the Dr. and Cr. Totals agree in amount the work may be regarded as right.

324. Journals may in like manner be arranged with *six* sets of money columns, — three for Drs. to Mdse., Cash, and Sundries, and three for Crs. to these accounts severally. The *principle* being understood, the manner of ruling and keeping the Journal may be adapted to the particular nature of one's business; and whatever may be the number of money columns in the Journal, on instituting a Proof, as indicated in the last article, the total amount from adding the sums in all the Dr. columns of a page, will exactly equal that from adding the sums in all the Cr. columns. (Art. 311.)

325. The learner will do well to write out a statement of Assets and Liabilities, and of the Transactions on which the following Illustrative Example is based, in accordance with the suggestion of Art. 320. This Example represents the business of a Private Banker in the interior, who receives deposits from his customers and furnishes them Drafts on the Mercantile Bank, which is located in a commercial city on the sea-board.

326. As Cash in the Sixth Form takes the place of Merchandise in the Fifth, no Inventory will be required before proceeding to close the Ledger. The daily Cash Balances of a Banker, are to his business what the Merchandise on the shelves of the Merchant is to the business of the latter. When the Banker's Cash Account is made up at the close of the day, his books should be in a condition to show the exact state of his business.

QUEST. **323.** How are Journal *Proofs* obtained? — **324.** How else may Journals be arranged? — **325.** What statement is the learner advised to prepare? (See Art. 320.) What does the Illustrative Example represent? — **326.** What is said of the relations of Cash and Mdse.? To what may the Cash Balances of the Banker be compared?

Detroit, June 1st, 1860. 1

Cash.	Dr.	Sund's.	Dr.	L. F.		Sund's.	Cr.	Cash.	Cr.
				1	Sundries To Stock	9100	00		
					For follow'g Assets				
2500	00			√	Cash in Safe .				
		3400	00	1	Mercantile Bank				
		2750	00	2	BillsRec. per B.B.				
		450	00	2	S. Wood owes				
					me on account				
					———— " ————				
		1600	00	1	Stock To Sundries				
				4	To Job Otis on acct.	360	00		
				5	" H. Smith " "	640	00		
				4	" R. Cook " "	600	00		
					—— *June 2d.* ——				
255	00			3	Cash To O. Rood	255	00		
		378	75	4	Job Otis				
				1	To Mercan. Bank	375	00		
				3	" Exchange . .	3	75		
560	00			3	Cash To O. Rood	560	00		
252	50			√	Cash				
				1	To Mercan. Bank	250	00		
				3	" Exchange . .	2	50		
		350	00	2	BillsRec. No.4, B.B.				
				√	To Cash			350	00
		2000	00	1	Mercantile Bank				
				√	To Cash			2000	00
3567	*50*				*Cash Bal. $1217.50*			*2350*	*00*
					—— *June 4th.* ——				
500	00			2	Cash To S. Wood	500	00		
475	00			4	Cash To Job Otis	475	00		
		404	00	5	H. Smith				
				1	To Mercan. Bank	400	00		
				3	" Exchange	4	00		
					—— *Proof.* ——				
4542	50	11332	75		Sundries	13525	25	2350	00
		4542	50		Cash	2350	00		
		15875	25		Totals	15875	25		

June 4th continued.

Cash.	Dr.	Sund's.	Dr.	L. F.		Sund's.	Cr.	Cash.	Cr.
360	00			2	Cash To S. Wood	360	00		
275	00			5	Cash To H. Smith	275	00		
		479	75	2	S. Wood				
				1	To Mercan. Bank	475	00		
				3	" Exchange .	4	75		
247	50			4	Cash To R. Cook	247	50		
279	75			√	Cash				
				2	To Bills Receivable, No. 3, B. B.	276	00		
				5	To Interest . .	3	75		
466	90			√	Cash (Western) .				
				1	To Mercan. Bank	460	00		
				3	" Exch. 1½ %	6	90		
		375	50	2	Bills Receivable, No. 5, B. B. . .				
				√	To Cash . . .			375	50
		127	20	2	S. Wood To Cash			127	20
1629	*15*				*Cash Bal. $3318.95*			*502*	*70*
					June 5th.				
2370	00			√	Cash				
				2	To Bills Receivable, No. 2, B. B.	2290	00		
				5	To Interest . .	80	00		
		2500	00	1	Mercantile Bank				
				√	To Cash . . .			2500	00
384	00			4	Cash To Job Otis	384	00		
265	88			3	Cash To O. Rood	265	88		
		461	57	3	O. Rood				
				1	To Mercan. Bank	457	00		
				3	" Exchange .	4	57		
300	00			√	Cash				
				2	To Mercan. Bank	175	00		
				3	" Exchange .	1	75		
				2	" S. Wood .	123	25		
					Proof.				
4949	03	3944	02		Sundries . . .	5890	35	3002	70
		4949	03		Cash	3002	70		
		8893	05		Totals	8893	05		

When the learner has posted the Illustrative Example journalized on pp. 221 and 222, he will be prepared to answer the following questions:

1st. What is the Trial Balance from this Journal?

2d. What are the final Ledger Balances?

3d. What has been the Net Gain in business?

TRIAL BALANCE.

Ans. 1st.

Dr.			*June 5th,* 1860.			Cr.
Mercan. Bank, 1	5308	00	Stock,	p. 1	7500	00
Bills Receivable, 2	909	50	Exchange,	p. 3	28	22
S. Wood, p. 2	73	70	O. Rood,	p. 3	619	31
Cash Balance	4138	83	Job Otis,	p. 4	840	25
			R. Cook,	p. 4	847	50
			H. Smith,	p. 5	511	00
			Interest,	p. 5	83	75
	10430	03			10430	03

LEDGER BALANCES.

Ans. 2d.

Dr.			*June 7th,* 1860.			Cr.
Mercan Bank, 1	5308	00	Stock,	p. 1	7611	97
Bills Receivable, 2	909	50	O. Rood,	p. 3	619	31
S. Wood, p. 2	73	70	Job Otis,	p. 4	840	25
Cash Balance	4138	83	R. Cook,	p. 4	847	50
			H. Smith,	p. 5	511	00
	10430	03			10430	03

Ans. 3d. Net Gain in business, $111.97.

OPENING AND CLOSING.

327. The first difficulty which the inexperienced book-keeper has to encounter consists in Opening the Journal so as to make the several accounts involved conform to the existing facts at the time of commencing a business. This done, the current entries required in recording ordinary business transactions are comparatively easy, and have already been sufficiently elucidated. His second and principal difficulty, however, consists in Closing the Ledger — a process by which all accounts that indicate gain or loss in trade are eliminated from the Ledger, and by which the results of the business, however complex it may have been, are exhibited in Ledger Balances. Of these the Dr. exhibit Assets, and the Cr. Net Stock and Liabilities. (Arts. 304, 309, and 311.)

EXAMPLES FOR PRACTICE.

328. For the purpose of increasing the familiarity of the learner with the more difficult work of Opening and Closing sets of books in conformity with the varied cases that may arise, the following additional Examples for Practice are here introduced.

EXAMPLE I. OPENING.

329. I enter upon a Grocery Business, with the following Assets and Liabilities, and open my books with a Stock Account.

ASSETS. I bring into trade 100 bbls. of Sugar, weighing 200 lbs. each, and 5 hhds. of Molasses, containing 63 gallons each. The sugar stands me in $5\frac{3}{4}$ c. per lb., and the molasses $27\frac{1}{3}$ c. per gallon. All other Merchandise I bring into trade is together worth, per Inventory, $21,375.50. I hold Benja-

QUEST. **327.** What is said of Opening the Journal? What is remarked of current entries in ordinary business? In what does the second and principal difficulty of the book-keeper consist? — **328.** For what are additional Examples for Practice introduced? — **329.** What is stated in Art. 329? Give the Journal entry required by my Assets. Give the entry for my Liabilities.

min Butler's accepted Sight Draft, in my favor, on Henry Paywell, for $2000.00, and a Note of Hand against O. H. Bradbury for $1200.00 due in 30 days. I have also $1500.00 in Cash, all of which I put into the business.

LIABILITIES. There is outstanding against me an accepted Draft made by Sam. Brown, in favor of John Hunter, for $475.37, payable 10 days after sight, and my Note given to J. O. Baker, or order, for $1500.00, payable in 60 days. I am also indebted in the sum of $255.75 to Byron Howard on book account.

Required to determine the following Particulars:

1st. The Journal entry for my *Assets.*

2d. The Journal entry for my *Liabilities.*

3d. The *Net Value of my Stock* in trade.

EXAMPLE II. CLOSING.

330. The business presented in the last Example (Art. 329) is conducted for the period of one year, during which time I buy and sell Merchandise, receive Moneys on Bills due me, pay Bills maturing against me, and deal in Real Estate. At the expiration of the year I take a Trial Balance, and an Inventory of Merchandise and Real Estate on hand, with the following results:

Dr. TRIAL BALANCE. *Cr.*

Dr.			Cr.		
Cash	3750	60	Bills Payable	3600	
Bills Receivable	3450	10	Homer Brown	1460	50
Real Estate	22460		Profit & Loss	280	75
Expenses	1526	30	Interest	260	60
H. K. Powers	573		Discount	825	50
Exchange	84	28	James Hill	1090	
Merchandise	753	55	Stock	25080	48
	32597	83		32597	83

QUEST. **330.** What is stated in Art. 330, and what is required?

INVENTORY. On taking an Inventory I find I have on hand Merchandise worth $11,376.80, and Real Estate worth $22,000.00.

1st. Required to eliminate from the Ledger all accounts indicating Gain or Loss in trade, and to present in their modified condition the final Ledger Balances. Of these the Drs. exhibit Assets, and the Crs. Net Stock and Liabilities. (Acts. 298 to 307.)

2d. Required the Net Gain in trade for one year.

Ans. 1.

Dr. LEDGER BALANCES. *Cr.*

Cash	3750	60	Bills Payable	3600	
Bills Receivable	3450	10	Homer Brown	1460	50
Real Estate	22000		James Hill	1090	
H. K. Powers	573		Stock	35000	
Merchandise	11376	80			
	41150	50		41150	50

Ans. 2. Net Gain in trade $9919.52.

EXAMPLE III. OPENING.

Partnership without Stock Account.

331. I associate with me Hiram Boomer, and continue the business of the last Example, under the style and title of "Mayhew & Boomer." * I put into the business my Assets, as they appear in the above Ledger Balances, with the exception of my Real Estate, the firm assuming my Liabilities; and Boomer brings in $12,500.00 in Cash, and $5500.00 in Merchandise. We are each to keep $15,000.00 in the business, as nearly as may be, and are entitled to receive

* See marginal reference on page 198.

QUEST. 331. Give the Journal entry required by Art. 331.

10% interest on the excess of our credits above this sum, and are each to allow the firm a like rate of interest for what our credits shall fall short of this sum, in case they fail to equal it. After interest to the partners has been entered, we are to share equally in the proceeds of the business. We open the books without a Stock account, the amount each partner has in trade being put to his Cr. in personal account.

Required the Opening Journal Entry.

EXAMPLE IV. CLOSING.

Partnership without Stock Account.

332. We continue the business introduced in the last Example for one year, when we take a Trial Balance and an Inventory, with the following results:

Dr. TRIAL BALANCE. *Cr.*

Cash	9875	50	Ira Mayhew	13000	
Bills Receivable	12940		Hiram Boomer	18000	
Expenses	1120		Bills Payable	4600	
Exchange	28	75	Interest	275	80
Merchandise	11911	55			
	35875	80		35875	80

INVENTORY. We have Merchandise worth, per Inventory, $15,373.00. Each partner's credits have remained unchanged.

1st. Required the Journal entries for Interest to the partners.

2d. Has there been *Gain* or *Loss* in trade, and how much?

3d. What sum stands to the Cr. of each partner on closing the Ledger Accounts?

332. Explain the process of closing required in Art. 332.

4th. What has been each partner's *Gain* or *Loss* in trade?

Ans. 2. There has been a *Gain* in trade of $2488.50.

Ans. 3. Ira Mayhew's Cr. $14,044.25. H. Boomer's Cr. $19,544.25.

Ans. 4. Ira Mayhew's Gain $1044.25. H. Boomer's Gain $1544.25.

IMPORTANCE OF THIS SCIENCE.

333. The student has seen that this work, which commences with the simplest elements of Book-keeping, in its progress gradually unfolds, illustrates, and applies, *principles*, the observance of which will enable practical accountants and business men systematically to record all kinds of mercantile and commercial transactions, so as to exhibit the results of each branch of a business, however varied and complex it may be, and so to keep their accounts, and take and enter their ledger balances, (monthly, or oftener, as their business shall require,) as to feel constantly assured that their books are free from errors, and to know at all times the exact state of their affairs. When one can thus see, at a glance, the source and amount of all gains and losses arising in his business, there is distinctly indicated to him what changes, if any, should be made in order to render it more safe and prosperous. This science, it will hence be seen, while valuable as a school study for discipline, is at the same time eminently worthy of the most careful consideration of practical men who would entertain reasonable hopes of success in business.

QUEST. **333.** What is said of the importance of Book-keeping as a study?

NOTE. In Transaction 73, at the 116th page, the Wool bought for Isaac Hill weighed, as purchased in small lots, 7292 lbs.; but when weighed out and accounted for, there was altogether only 7281 lbs. Commission, in such cases, is allowed only on the amount as weighed out when shipped.

www.ingramcontent.com/pod-product-compliance
Lightning Source LLC
LaVergne TN
LVHW050528100826
845148LV00002B/476

* 9 7 8 1 4 2 5 5 1 9 2 2 3 *